The Berkshire Photo Album

Historic Images — 1870s-1990s

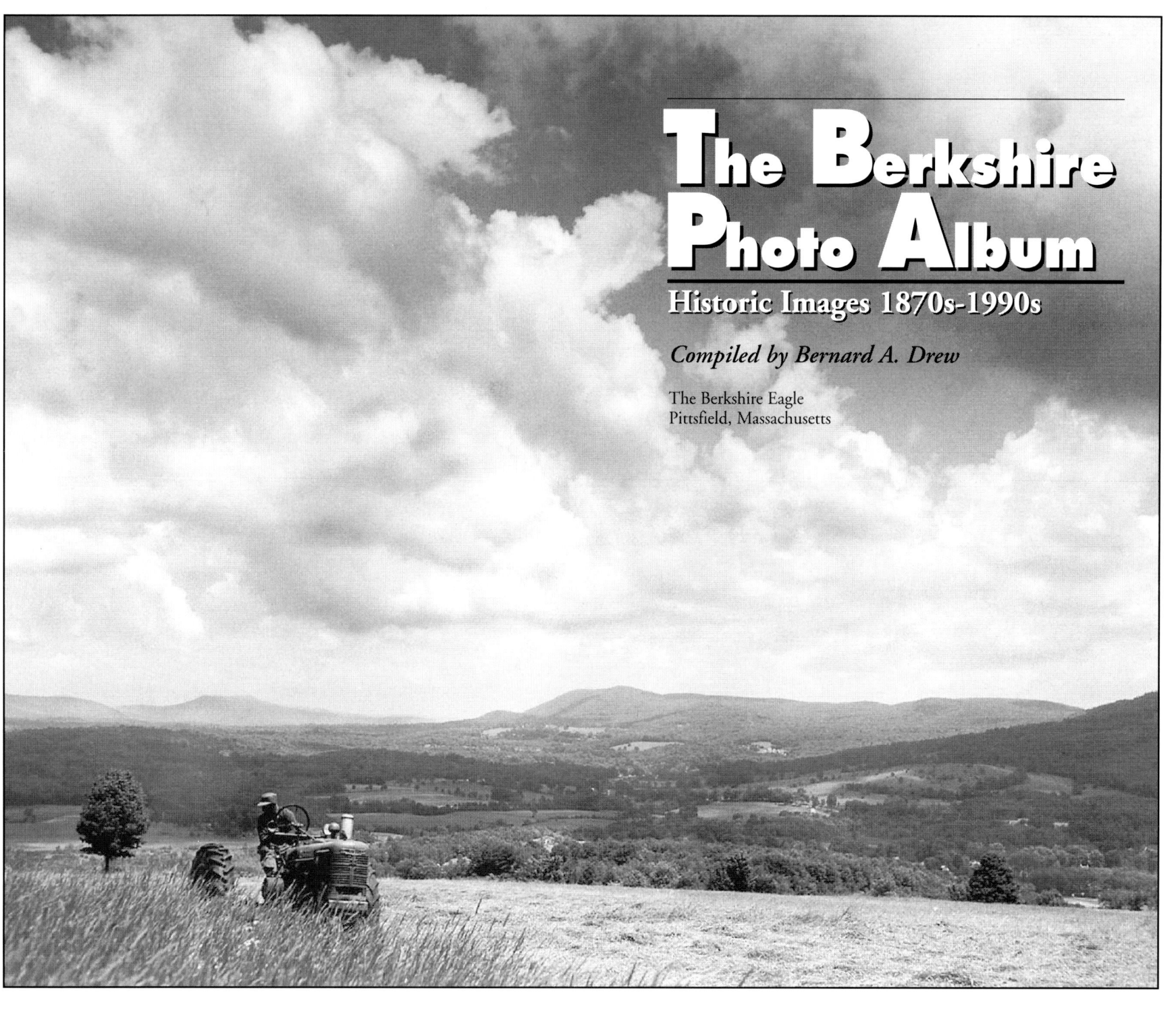

The Berkshire Photo Album

Historic Images 1870s-1990s

Compiled by Bernard A. Drew

The Berkshire Eagle
Pittsfield, Massachusetts

Copyright © 1999 Bernard A. Drew and
New England Newspapers, Inc.

All rights reserved
Printed by Eagle Printing, Binding & Mailing, Pittsfield, Massachusetts

No part of this publication may be reproduced, stored in a retrieval system or transmitted in any form or by any means (electronic, mechanical, photocopying, recorded or other) without prior written permission of the publisher, except for review purposes or for brief, credited citation.

Library of Congress Catalog Card Number: 99-61640
ISBN 0-9671427-0-9

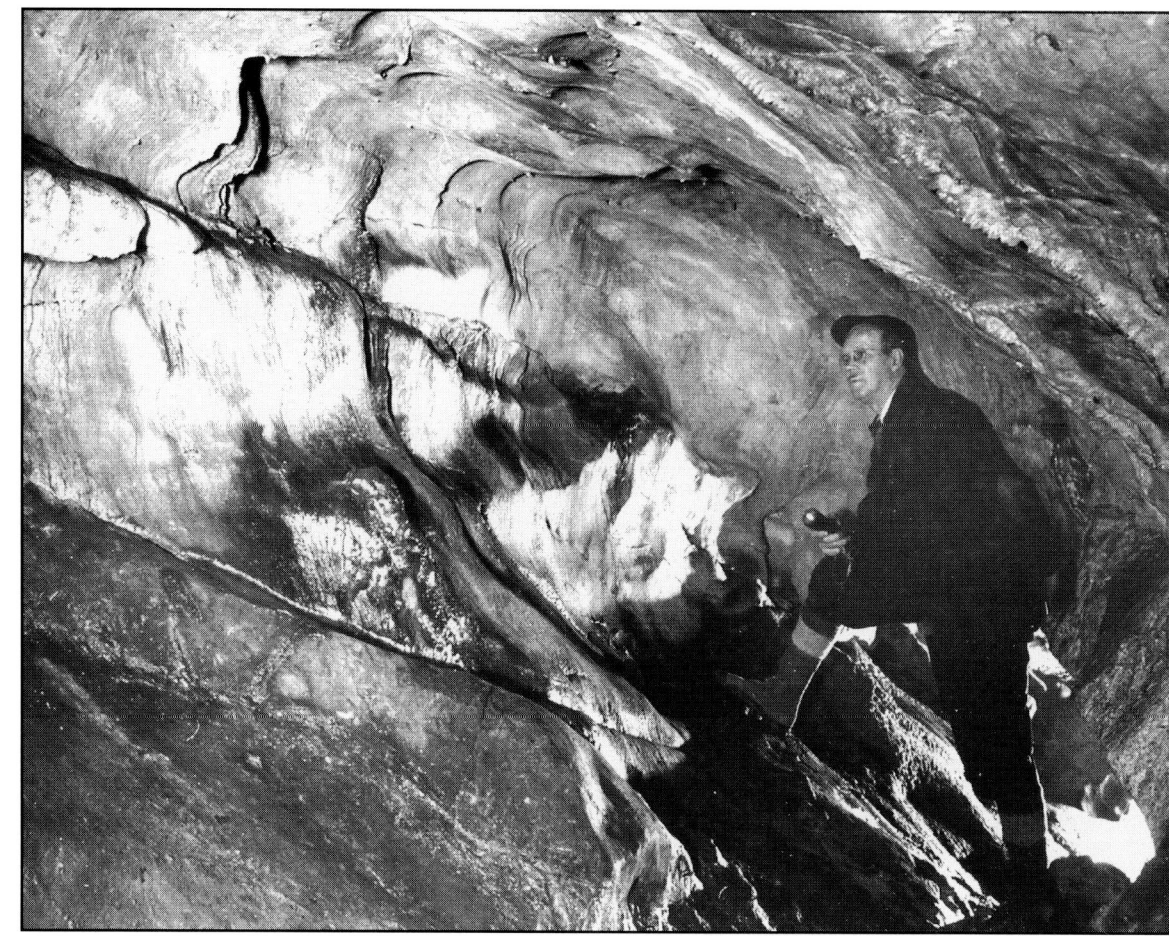

Front cover: Members of the Maynard family relax at home in Dalton with their reading in 1898—see Pages 66 & 67. (*Dwight M. Maynard collection, courtesy Raymond W. Fischer*) **Title page:** There is a threatening sky over Maple Hill in West Stockbridge in 1955. (*Kingsley R. Fall/Berkshire Eagle*) **This page:** Clair W. "Clay" Perry (1887-1961) explores Baker's Quarry Cave (known for its red-headed bats) in Lanesboro. An ardent cave crawler, Perry coined the word "spelunker" and wrote the popular *Under Ground New England*. (*William H. Tague, Berkshire Eagle, circa 1953*) **Next page:** A group romps atop Mount Greylock in 1905, a camera handy to record the occasion. (*Berkshire Eagle collection*) **Back cover:** A huge staging shrouds England Brothers on Pittsfield's North Street as the department store is enlarged in 1925-26. Edith Babcock operates a machine at Pittsfield's General Electric in 1943. (*Both Berkshire Eagle collection*)

Acknowledgements: The author thanks Martin C. Langeveld for suggesting this book; Grace McMahon for blazing a trail through *The Berkshire Eagle*'s clippings and photo files; Gary Leveille for reading the manuscript and making many good suggestions; the many people who are named throughout these pages for loaning photos; and especially those who over the years have taken the time to write names and dates on the backs of pictures.

Introduction

"The habit of looking at men in the gross makes their lives have less of human interest for us. But though there are crowds of laborers before us, yet each one leads his little epic life each day."
— *Henry David Thoreau, journal entry, 11 September 1851*

The woodland philosopher's observation pretty much sums up the intent of this historical album: it celebrates through small examples aggregate tenacity, creativity and individuality of the inhabitants of Massachusetts' westernmost county.

Photos are grouped in more than eighty-five topics, from *The Lafayette* on Pontoosuc Lake to the Whitney Estate on October Mountain; from the Trzepacz family in its Pittsfield grocery to rattlesnake stalker Ike Whitbeck in Mount Washington. Some subject choices are obvious, such as farms or baseball or textile mills. Many are of enduring interest, such as General Electric, Mount Greylock or England Brothers. And a few, such as giant vegetables, pond floaters and border flirts, are admittedly whimsical.

Three photographers provide fascinating glimpses of their families and their villages circa 1890-1910, the advent of amateur picture taking: Dwight M. Maynard in Dalton, Carrie Smith Lorraine in Sheffield and Frank E. Sisson in Mill River. Thanks to Truman B. Stearns, we see Civilian Conservation Corpsmen at work at Pittsfield State Forest one winter. Through David Milton Jones' pictures, we watch Stockbridge and Lee firemen relax at a clambake. And with Fred W. Sauer's views, we follow construction of the Glendale dam and powerhouse.

All photos are credited as to source—besides the *Eagle*'s large archive, pictures were borrowed from organizations and private collections—and as possible, to camera artist. You'll recognize the names of several professional portraitists and experienced *Eagle* staff photographers within these pages, and perhaps some of the talented amateurs as well.

—Bernard A. Drew

Apples

A is for Apple, B is for... Arcade J. Bartlett (1901-86) **[A]**, who contemplates his 1970 crop at the family orchard in Richmond. Bartlett and his wife Sophie (1909-85) purchased the former Arthur Howard farm in 1947 and with son and daughter-in-law Francis A. and Betty Bartlett set up a small roadside stand on Swamp Road. The Bartletts in 1958 built a concrete cold storage facility with cider-making room and retail area, then expanded the facility a second time in 1970. By then, Arcade's grandsons Rick and Ron were active in the business. (*Ruth Bass/Berkshire Eagle*)

C is for Cider, D is for... Charles H. "Charlie" Daniels (1859-1937) **[B]**, standing second from right. A certified character, Daniels dabbled in politics. He was a musician. And he was an apple squeezer of some repute. His mill on Hancock Road near the junction of Peck's Road in Pittsfield pressed an estimated 5,000 gallons a week, at the height of the autumn season. Daniels suffered a respiratory ailment which kept him from lying down. But it did not prevent him from telling a tall tale or two to welcome visitors. Daniels' real estate holdings included land on Potter Mountain which he eventually sold to the Commonwealth of Massachusetts and is now part of Pittsfield State Forest. (*Berkshire Eagle collection*)

Farming

Farming is cyclical work. Hired hands unload wagons of hay into a barn at Pinecroft in Lenox in summer [A]. Mr. and Mrs. Peter Augustus Schermerhorn, members of an old and wealthy New York family and among the earliest of the summer social set in Lenox, purchased Pinecroft in 1853. (*Berkshire Eagle collection, Edwin Hale Lincoln photo*)

Come spring, it is time to spread a winter's accumulation of manure on the fields, as these North Adams farmers are doing [B]. (*Berkshire Eagle collection, Roger Johnson plate*)

Willowbrook Dairy on Miller Avenue in Sheffield **[C]**, destroyed by fire and rebuilt in 1910, remained active until 1938. Besides bottling milk, it made cheese. George Patterson was long-time manager. The building was used to house town machinery when it burned a second time in 1962. (*Sheffield Historical Society collection*)

Farming offered a welcome opportunity for independence to emigrants such as Patrick J. Hughes (1849-1915) **[D]**, who was born in County Mayo, Ireland, and came to the United States in 1868 with only the shirt on his back. He worked as a hand on the Hewins farm in Sheffield, eventually saving enough to purchase his own place. Hughes raised horses, milked cows and grew acres of onions, cabbage, squash and other vegetables which he peddled by horse and wagon. He married Mary Conneally, with whom he had two children, and, after her death, Ellen Agnes Ruane (1856-1915) **[E]**, with whom he had four more children.

(*Sheffield Historical Society collection*)

Farms experienced a severe labor shortage during World War I. College girls were recruited to help. Here two "farmerettes" **[F]** are at John E. and Mary D. Parsons' Stoneover Farm in Lenox. (*Berkshire Eagle collection*)

Berkshire's first "hippie" farmer was Albert Franklin "O.B. Joyful" Tyler (1872-1969) **[G]**, a bearded vegetarian who never touched tea, coffee, sugar, salt, tobacco, alcohol or milk. A homespun philosopher, Tyler's business card stated his name and the fee of a dollar per question. (*Berkshire Eagle collection*)

A. Wallace Tryon (1894-1994) [H], a veteran of World War I, operated a livery and garage business in Monterey and also the Tryon Tea Room. Here he gathers maple sap in spring to boil into syrup. (*Berkshire Eagle collection*)

George H. Kirchoff (1877-1956) [I] and his field crew are ready to blow chopped corn into the silo. Kirchoff and his wife Clotilde farmed on State Road in Great Barrington beginning in 1912. (*Courtesy Patricia Holohan*)

Lewis E. Barlow [J], a fourth generation farmer in East Lee, had one horse and no auto in the late 1920s. "Oxen are fast enough for me and they are more profitable than a Ford," he said. "I bought a pair for $150 and sold them four years later for $280. With a Ford, it would be just the opposite, only more so." (*Berkshire Eagle collection, C.S. Hayward photo*)

The Pierce family for many years operated a flour, grain, coal and farmers' supply store at the corner of Main and Maple Streets in Hinsdale (the building is still there). Shown in this 1929 view [K] are, from left, John McGill, Carlton A. Pierce, Pierce's grandsons Carlton H. and Douglas F. and his son Carl A. (1892-1945), who in 1923 succeeded him in operating the business. (*Courtesy Doug and Nicole Pierce*)

Old-fashioned horse draws have long been an attraction at country fairs including Middlefield's [L], which began its annual cattle show tradition in 1855. (*Berkshire Eagle collection, S.R. Kanter photo*)

Herdsmen

Arthur J. Coons [A] of Great Barrington said there were six or seven dairymen in town when he started his farm in 1950. Now there are only two. He and a son today manage a herd of about 140 animals. (*Joel Librizzi/Berkshire Eagle, 1989*)

John B. Watson [B], born in Perthshire, Scotland, leased a gristmill and farm on Lord Lansdowne's estate before emigrating to the United States in 1888. Spotting an advertisement for an inexpensive, run-down farm in the town of Washington, he settled here and raised thoroughbred Shetland ponies—the only one to do so in Massachusetts—in the 1920s. (*Berkshire Eagle collection*)

William S. Noble (1852-1936) imported $50 worth of Louisiana bullfrogs and stocked a pond on his farm on outer East Street, Pittsfield. He claimed the amphibians would grow to 22 inches in length, nose to toe, with meaty and edible forearms as well as rear legs. Noble fenced the pond to keep his herd in, and poachers out. Noble had a dairy route and also maintained water towers for the nearby Boston & Albany Railroad. Neither Noble nor his frogs would pose for a photographer when a *Berkshire Evening Eagle* reporter visited in June 1934. The croaker pictured [C], resident of a Lenox pond, may or may not be a descendant of Noble's herd. (*Berkshire Eagle collection, Roger S. Hart photo*)

Giant Vegetables

A man and his son resort to axes to harvest this unlikely cabbage in Mill River in 1909. Postcard publishers had a laugh, thanks to a little darkroom manipulation, publishing photo cards of over-sized animals or giant vegetables **[A]**. (*Berkshire County Historical Society collection*)

But ninety years later, one wonders. Joe Goetze, left **[B]**, stands with the 1,000-pound-or-so pumpkin grown in his garden on Vinal Drive in Pittsfield. (*Ben Garver/Berkshire Eagle, 1998*)

Mount Hope Farm

Col. Ezra Parmalee Prentice (1863-1955) **[A]**, lawyer, cattle and poultry breeder, author and owner of the 1,500-acre Mount Hope Farm in Williamstown, conducted experiments to improve milk production and butterfat content in dairy cattle. One cow, Mount Hope Faithful, broke a ten-year record by producing 19,206.5 pounds of milk with 977.62 pounds of butterfat over 365 days in 1935. Mount Hope Queen **[B]**, was one of Prentice's experimental cluckers. Prentice employed a farm and domestic staff of 168 people, two of them full-time geneticists. Three orchards of 1,000 trees produced some 22,000 bushels of apples each autumn.

Prentice's wife Alta (1871-1962), daughter of oil baron John D. Rockefeller Sr., was an accomplished musician. She was active in a charitable endeavors including the founding of a settlement house, known as the Alta House, in the Italian quarter of Cleveland.

Following Mrs. Prentice's death, the property went through several owners. A group of Williams College alumni acquired Mount Hope Farm **[C]**, including the three-story Georgian-style Elm Tree House, in 1985 for $1.64 million and donated it to the college, which is using the main building for educational programs. (*All Berkshire Eagle Collection*)

A nature walker stops for a lunch at Bartholomew's Cobble **[A]**. Designated a National Natural Landmark in 1971, the 277-acre preserve in the Ashley Falls section of Sheffield is a property of the Trustees of Reservations. It was named for its original owner, George Bartholomew (1808-69), who used it as cow pasture for many years. More than 800 species of plants have been catalogued here, including 500 wildflowers, 100 trees, shrubs and vines and fifty-three ferns and fern allies. (*Berkshire Eagle collection, Arthur Palme photo*)

Alvah W. Sanborn feeds a baby rabbit at Pleasant Valley Wildlife Sanctuary in Lenox **[B]**. A property of the Massachusetts Audubon Society, the sanctuary was created in 1928 when Mary Parsons (1862-1940) of Lenox formed a group to purchase the 200-acre former Michael Power farm. Sanborn, an ornithologist and nature photographer, headed the sanctuary from 1946-73. (*Berkshire Eagle collection, Warren Fowler photo*)

Lt. Col. Arthur D. Budd (1882-1965) **[C]**, a West Point graduate, earned a Distinguished Service Cross for heroism in World War I action near Grand Pré, France, in October 1918. He retired to a country barony in Windsor. He bequeathed his 3,000 acres of former farmlands, Notchview, to the Trustees of Reservations. The property is open to the public today for hiking and cross-country skiing. Budd was fond of dogs, and often had more than a dozen mixed breeds in his kennel. (*Courtesy Warren A. Drew*)

Mount Greylock

Mount Greylock Reservation, acquired by the Commonwealth of Massachusetts in 1898, now encompasses some 10,327 acres. Pittsfield lawyer and Congressman Francis Rockwell (1844-1929), who chaired the Mount Greylock Commission from 1910-29, visits the summit with a group of journalists in 1906 **[A]**, when a new south access (Rockwell Road) was proposed. Until that road was built in the early 1930s, the main approach was from the northerly Notch Road. (*Berkshire Eagle collection*)

Williams College erected wooden observation towers on Greylock in 1830 and '41. The Greylock Park Association in 1885 constructed a more durable metal structure, which in turn was replaced by the granite World War I memorial tower. Designed by Maginnis and Walsh of Boston, it is seen under construction in 1932 **[B]**. (*Berkshire Eagle collection, Arthur Palme photo*)

Laurence Estes (1898-1981) **[C]** of Dalton, an employee of the state Department of Public Works, stands on the porch of the first small summit house, which was built in 1875. (*Berkshire Eagle collection, courtesy Drusilla Estes*) The lodge burned in 1929. With the help of the Civilian Conservation Corps, a new structure **[D]** designed by Pittsfield architect Joseph McA. Vance was completed in 1935. (*Berkshire Eagle collection*) Named Bascom Lodge, after long-time Commission member and Williams College professor John Bascom (1827-1911), the new summit house affords lodging for hikers and has a small restaurant and store. This is the dining room in 1983 **[E]**. (*Susan Plageman/Berkshire Eagle*)

Philip D. Powers of Adams is said to have been the first to drive by car to the top of Mount Greylock in winter, in about 1917. But only snowmobiles such as the Massachusetts State Police vehicle **[F]**, seen in 1949, guaranteed year-round access. (*Berkshire Eagle collection, Edward A. Sivik photo*)

And nothing beat foot power. Naturalist Henry David Thoreau (1817-62) ambled to the top of Greylock in 1844 to spend a chilly night, and hikers on the Appalachian Trail—which was built over the mountain in 1928—still climb it in large numbers today. Some 1,500 people take part in the annual Greylock Ramble in autumn 1978 **[G]**. (*Joel Librizzi/Berkshire Eagle*)

William C. Whitney (1841-1904) as a lawyer fought the Tweed Ring in New York City and during President Grover Cleveland's first term was Secretary of the Navy. The millionaire secretly acquired mountaintop acreage in the town of Washington in 1896 and hired carpenters to build a rural retreat called Antlers, shown under construction **[A]**, (*Lenox Library collection*) and after completion **[B]**. (*Berkshire Eagle collection, C.S. Hayward photo*)

Whitney fenced part of his vast, 14,000-acre preserve and stocked it with game birds, elk, bison and moose **[C]**. (*Berkshire Eagle collection, C.S. Hayward photo*) Old Bill the moose, named for sympathetic Game Warden William W. Sargood (1860-1942), escaped the Whitney property and roamed the woods for years, until shot illegally by a hunter in 1920. Sargood had the head mounted and it hangs today in the Berkshire Museum in Pittsfield **[D]**. (*Bernard Drew photo*)

Whitney had a honeymoon cottage constructed for use by his son Harry Payne Whitney and his new bride Gertrude Vanderbilt **[E]**. (*Courtesy Leona A. Butler*) After the death of his wife Edith in 1899, the senior Whitney lost interest in the property. Through efforts of *Berkshire Eagle* publisher Kelton B. Miller (1860-1941), Cortlandt Field Bishop and others, Massachusetts acquired the land and called it October Mountain State Forest in 1921. Three Civilian Conservation Corps camps were based in or near the forest during the 1930s. Now gone, the shingle-sided, 81-foot water tower at Antlers **[F]** was one of the last reminders of the country estate. (*Berkshire Eagle collection*)

Whitney Estate

State Forests

Berkshire boasts more than two dozen state forests, including Bash Bish Falls in Mount Washington, a winter wonderland in the scene from 1941 **[A]**. Photographer Arthur Palme (1884-1949), a native of Austria and later a resident of Pittsfield, was an engineer with General Electric. His wife Edith M. Palme (1893-1986) is the one shown on skis. (*Berkshire Eagle collection, Arthur Palme*)

The versical Mount Washington sisters Elaine (1863-1953) and Dora Read Goodale (1866-1953) were widely known as the "Apple Blossom Poets" after their first book struck a popular chord in 1878. The family's now-gone Sky Farm **[B]** is part of Mount Washington State Forest today. (*Author's collection*)

Natural Bridge in North Adams **[C]**, a calcium carbonate formation, was discovered by Mohawk Indians and by Seth Hudson, a hunter at Fort Massachusetts in the early 1700s. Maintained as a tourist attraction for many years by Edward J. Elder (1903-84), it was sold in 1985 to the Department of Environmental Management, which operates it as a state park today. (*William H. Tague/Berkshire Eagle, 1957*)

Earle Stafford (1887-1976) **[D]**, a professional landscape architect, was resident forester at Arthur Warton Swann State Forest in Monterey from 1921-41, developing Massachusetts' first experimental forest and creating large plantations of spruce and other species. The land was given to the commonwealth in 1918 by Susan Ridley Sedgwick Swann (1886-1981). It is named for her husband, who as a boy hunted the property and, after becoming a physician, died in 1914 at the age of thirty-four. (*Courtesy Gordon Stafford*)

CCC

Franklin D. Roosevelt's "forest army," the Civilian Conservation Corps, was doubly beneficial: Active from 1933-42, it jump-started a Depression-ravaged economy and it developed Massachusetts' fledgling state forest system. There were fourteen CCC camps and one veteran's camp in Berkshire County, scattered from Otis and Becket to Monroe and Greylock. Each camp had military and civilian supervisors. The crew based at Pittsfield State Forest is seen at work during the winter of 1933-34 at the upper dam, Lulu Cascade **[A]**; hauling wood **[B]**; and erecting a foot bridge near the barracks **[C]**. (*All Berkshire Eagle collection, courtesy Truman B. Stearns*)

That may be Truman B. Stearns (1881-1954) [D], superintendent of Pittsfield State Forest and supervisor of the CCC crews, inspecting a pond excavation in November 1933. Workers pose at a root cellar [E] and clear a roadway [F]. (*All Berkshire Eagle collection, courtesy Truman B. Stearns*)

The CCC administration building at Pittsfield State Forest [G] was restored as part of the Department of Environmental Management's 1998 celebration of the Massachusetts parks system's centennial. At a ceremony in October 1998, Division of Parks and Forests Region 5 Director Douglas Polland, standing at microphone, introduces Col. Lawrence Carlberg, seated at right. Carlberg, captain of the Pittsfield CCC 127 from 1935-41, said the group's accomplishments included building a road from Lulu Cascades to Berry Pond, creating the Ghost and Shadow ski trails and erecting a ski lodge. Decorated for his service in North Africa during World War II, Carlberg retired from the Air Force in 1959. (*Bernard Drew photo*)

Hunting

Robert A. Haskins (d. 1969) of Savoy displays a 22.5-pound raccoon which he and his dog Jack killed in 1931 **[A]**. Jack, disdaining publicity, turns his back. Haskins worked for Brightwater Co., then L.L. Brown Paper, both in Adams, and also drove a school bus. (*Berkshire Eagle collection, C.S. Hayward photo*)

Laurence T. Harris (1897-1949) of Lenox, center, and his son Laurence F., left, trapped seventy-two foxes in the first two weeks of the season in 1949) **[B]**. Second son Irving E., right, sat in for the picture but wasn't yet a trapper. At the time, the Pittsfield Sportsmen's Club offered a $5 bounty per skin. Miller J. Rhinehart, owner of a turkey farm in Lanesboro, paid Harris $3 per skin when the latter trapped fifteen foxes that were menacing his birds. (*Berkshire Eagle collection, C.S. Hayward photo*)

An interesting figure in this photograph **[C]** of a circa 1900 hunting party is the African-American orderly accompanying the group. (*Berkshire Eagle collection*)

Scouts

Franklin L. "Cap" Couch (1892-1979) **[A]**, a grandson of Dalton papermaker Zenas Crane and veteran of two world wars, was a longtime scout leader and Congregational minister. In the late 1930s, his Troop 4 in Dalton was recognized as the largest Boy Scout troop in the world. Couch in 1934 launched *The Village Press*, a weekly newspaper, and worked as personnel director for Crane & Co. He was recalled to active duty in 1943, serving in the Philippines, finally retiring in 1950 from the Army Reserves with the rank of colonel. He took to the pulpit and served Tyringham Union Church until 1973. (*Berkshire Eagle collection*)

Two Boy Scout patrols smile for the camera in Lanesboro in about 1915 **[B]**. (*Courtesy Martin C. Langeveld*)

Members of Pittsfield's first Girl Scouts troup have their picture taken. **[C]**. (*Berkshire Eagle collection*)

Illustrator Norman Rockwell (1894-1978) **[D]** — one of the few American artists with an entire museum devoted to his works, in his adopted town Stockbridge—unveils his latest Boy Scouts of America calendar painting in Pittsfield in 1962. (*Courtesy the photographer, Art Marasco*)

Camping

Campers tote sleeping bags to their cabins at Camp Witawentin day camp in 1943 **[A]** (*Berkshire Eagle*). Located at various times on Richmond Pond, Plunkett Reservoir and Onota Lake, and operated by the Girls League, Witawentin first opened in about 1914. Another group of campers in 1950 makes nature crafts **[B]**. (*Will Plouffe/Berkshire Eagle*)

The Boys' Club's Camp Russell on Richmond Pond stresses hygiene as part of it's daily routine in 1946 **[C]**. Washing up are Robert O'Brien, David Helliwell, Peter Genovese and Robert Lee. After rub-a-dub-dub it's on to the grub! Boys devour their lunches at the same camp in 1945 **[D]**. (*Both Berkshire Eagle*)

Walter Prichard Eaton (1878-1957) and his wife Elise Morris Underhill (d. 1969) camp at Crater Lake in Oregon [E]. Longtime drama critic and professor at Yale University, Eaton lived in Stockbridge and later Sheffield. His novel *The Idyl of Twin Fires* (1914) inspired a brief back-to-the-country movement while his *Boy Scouts of Berkshire* (1912) and sequels, chronicling the adventures of the Chipmunk Patrol, delighted a generation of young readers. (*Sheffield Historical Society collection, Fred H. Kiser/Kiser's Studio*).

Seymour Lipkin, a Tanglewood pianist and conductor of the Berkshire Music Center, directs student musicians at the Indian Hill Music Workshop in Stockbridge in 1954 [F]. (*Berkshire Eagle*)

This trio is obviously enjoying the summer cottage life [G]. (*Lee Library collection*) Even without clothes, this young patron in mother's arms has worked up a sweat at Birch Acres nudist camp in Hancock in 1983 and needs a Popsicle [H]. (*Warren Fowler/Berkshire Eagle*)

Fishing

They obviously have the right bait. Matthew Morrison (1867-1922) fishes in Upper Cone Brook, Richmond, in about 1905-06 **[A]**. Morrison was overseer of the spinning room at W.E. Tillotson Co. on Silver Lake in Pittsfield. (*Berkshire Eagle collection, courtesy David Donald*)

Louis Zwinglestein (1896-1974) of Melville Street, Pittsfield, a heavy-equipment operator for the city, pulls a pickerel from Onota Lake in December 1942 **[B]**. (*Berkshire Eagle*)

Housatonic River

German-born engineer Fritz Von Emperger (1862-1942) designed one of the most unusual bridges to span the Housatonic River. Commissioned by Stockbridge's Laurel Hill Association, his 1894 footbridge connecting Laurel Hill and Ice Glen was a memorial to association founder Mary Hopkins Goodrich (1814-95). Made of reinforced concrete, the span was a major technological innovation [A] even if it did collapse of its own weight just before it was finished in May 1895. It had to be rebuilt. As years passed, the structure deteriorated and was finally condemned in 1931. It was replaced five years later by the present suspension bridge designed by Joseph Franz. (*Author's collection*)

Built in the 1950s, this covered bridge [B] — one of two in Sheffield when this picture was taken — was damaged by an overweight truck and was torn down in 1988, replaced by a concrete and steel structure. (*Tom Bleezarde/Berkshire Eagle*)

The only time Viking women were known to have paddled on a Berkshire stream was in August 1991 [C] as part of the Housatonic River Flotilla, a waterway celebration held in Great Barrington. The Norse heroines are, from left, Pat Pixley, Belle Fox-Martin, Robin Sterling and Cheryl Hutto. Rachel Fletcher, who organized the river event, has directed Great Barrington's volunteer-made-and-maintained River Walk for more than a decade. (*Craig F. Walker/Berkshire Eagle, courtesy Rachel Fletcher*)

The Lafayette on Pontoosuc Lake

Large-scale recreation on Pontoosuc Lake in Pittsfield began with Peter Hodecker's launching of *The Lafayette* in 1889 **[A & B]**. The double-decker craft carried as many as 300 passengers who were brought to the dock by horse-drawn trolleys. (*Both Berkshire Eagle collection, given by Randy Trabold*)

Hodecker (1846-1939) **[C]**, a native of Alsace Lorraine, constructed the steamer himself at a cost of $7,000, using oak lumber and a power plant discarded from the Pontoosuc Woolen Mill, where he once worked. After twenty-two accident-free years, Hodecker dismantled his boat and used the materials to build small cabins along the lake. He placed the pilot house over a well near his house. The "captain" retired and took up golf. (*Berkshire Eagle collection, C.S. Hayward photo, 1920*)

Pond Floaters

Lily pads on Onota Lake [A] create a charming, natural vista in 1991. (*Craig F. Walker/Berkshire Eagle*) But there's a disconcerting similarity in a view [B] of a tire-choked cove on the Housatonic River in Sheffield. The graveyard for junk autos as well as bald rubber was found to be in violation of the Hatch Act in 1968 and was ordered cleaned up. (*Corea/Berkshire Eagle*)

Foliage

A rite of autumn: leaf raking. Entitled "Would You Be-Leave a Million," this photo **[A]** won a UPI photography contest in 1967. (*Joel Librizzi/Berkshire Eagle*)

Stockbridge Tree Warden Thomas F. Killfoile (1886-1940) didn't anticipate the public outcry when he held a public hearing in February 1932 and proposed toppling a large tree on Elm Street in front of the new post office. The Laurel Hill Association, the country's earliest village improvement society, was among loud objectors. As a result, the tree was dug up and moved to a safer location **[B]**. (*Stockbridge Library Association Historical Collection, David Milton Jones photo, thanks to Barbara Allen*)

Bicycling

Bicycling fever gripped the region in the 1890s. Members of the North Adams Bicycle Club **[A]** line up with their high-wheelers. (*Berkshire Eagle collection, courtesy J. Fred Walden Jr.*) Henry Robarge (1862-1948), left, and Dennis "Denny" Haylon (1868-1939) **[B]** are among the last surviving members to attend a Pittsfield Bicycle Club reunion in 1938. The club had been active until World War I. Robarge, an ambidextrous barber, served on the Pittsfield Common Council and was an amateur photographer. Haylon, who worked for *The Berkshire Eagle* for forty-eight years and became managing editor, was also treasurer of the Eastern Baseball League from 1919-30 and was one of the original members of the city's Parks Commission from 1913-32. (*Berkshire Eagle collection*)

Youth hostelers **[C]** depart on an excursion from Mrs. Woodward Wilbur's boarding house in Lanesboro in August 1940. (*Berkshire Eagle collection*)

Horses

The original "horse power" was vital to early Berkshire transportation. Driver Hiram G. Gibson is at the reins of an express wagon in North Adams in 1887 **[A]**. (*Berkshire Eagle collection, courtesy Randy Trabold*)

Samuel L. Clemens (1835-1910) **[B]**, seated, alias Mark Twain, didn't have a lot to laugh about during his summer 1904 visit to Tyringham, the guest of *Century* magazine editor Richard Watson Gilder (1844-1909). Clemens' beloved wife Olivia (1845-1904) had just died. And his daughter Jean (1880-1909), who accompanied Clemens to the Berkshires, was injured in a fall from a horse frightened by a trolley in South Lee. (*Berkshire Eagle collection*)

As a lucky token, it had failed its first owner. But Herbert E. Moore (1867-1938) **[C]**, superintendent of Gilder's Four Brooks Farms, kept one of the aluminum horseshoes from Jean Clemens' Italian mount following the accident and nailed it over his door. (*Berkshire Eagle collection, C.S. Hayward photo, 1932*)

West Stockbridge native Patrick Fallon (1863-1924) operated a blacksmith shop on McKay Street in Pittsfield **[D]**. Nick Lamoreaux is standing next to the horse, the others are unknown. (*Berkshire Eagle collection, courtesy Gus Schnopp*)

Frank Sherill of Richmond takes boarding house guests for a pleasant ride on tree-shrouded Bird Sanctuary Road in 1908 **[E]**. (*Berkshire Eagle collection, Matthew Morrison photo courtesy David Donald*)

Motorcycles

"Big Bill" Stevens [A] is astride a Flying Merkle motorcycle at his Parker Street, Pittsfield, residence, in 1910-12 while Lester Avery of Union Street poses [B] with his Excelsior machine in 1913. (*Both Berkshire Eagle collection*)

Motorcyclists line up in front of Fred P. Cloutier Jr.'s shop on West Street, Pittsfield [C]. The Harley-Davidson agent offered "a full line of parts for all makes of machines and everything to equip the rider," according to a 1920 advertisement. (*Berkshire Eagle collection, W.H. Benedict photo*)

Automobiles

Early Berkshire motorists didn't hesitate to drive the most difficult terrain. Albert V. Phillips (1876-1946) **[A]** is at the wheel of a Chandler motor car—one of several makes he sold at his Pittsfield dealership—navigating the Big Cut near Greylock summit in October 1915. Passengers include A.J. Peacock and Clay Perry. (*Berkshire Eagle collection*)

An indefatigable innovator, Cortland Field Bishop (1870-1935) **[B]** of The Maples in Lenox mounted skis to the front of his imported French auto, and tracks to the rear to enable snow travel. Still, the vehicle failed in a 1917 assault on Mount Greylock. Halfway up the mountain, Bishop drove full speed into a snow bank. The car stalled, wouldn't start and couldn't be budged. The party wallowed back down the mountain and summoned help. Bishop wasn't having any better luck when this picture was snapped; W.J. Welsh, Lenox highway superintendent, is pushing Bishop's track car up Belden Hill on West Street in Lenox. (*Berkshire Eagle collection, courtesy Mary Capps*)

Another Bishop—Kenneth G. Bishop (1902-68) **[C]** of Clarksburg—in May 1922 purchased a new Model A Ford from Van Sleet Motor Co. on Ashland Street in North Adams for $498.65 (plus $3 extra for a foot accelerator). Bishop, a mule spinner at the Strong & Hewitt woolen mill, immediately sold the stock body and mounted a racing body on the chassis, according to his son Donald. (*Courtesy Donald G. Bishop*)

Muddy, twisting, steep Jacob's Ladder in Becket **[D]** was a motorist's nightmare before the new state highway was built in 1913. Gray-bearded Deacon Daniel Camp (1842-1911) **[E]** lived on the east side of the summit. When mired motorists came to him for help, he hitched his oxen and drew their vehicles to the top of the hill—for a fee. (*Berkshire Eagle collection*)

Cars were made of stronger materials than carriages or wagons, but still didn't last forever. A wind storm in Pittsfield in 1950 squashed this Cadillac **[F]**. (*Will Plouffe/Berkshire Eagle*), while a wrecker hauls away a loser in a Seymour Street mishap, probably in the early 1930s. **[G]**. (*Berkshire Eagle collection*)

Thomas Buckley pumped Socony gasoline at his Beaver Street Store in North Adams **[H]**, where four-year-old Donald G. Bishop poses with his aunt, Dorothy Griffin Ledger, in 1928. The building is now gone, Bishop said. (*Courtesy Donald G. Bishop*)

The town of Windsor acquired its first school bus, a Model T Ford [I], in 1920. Joseph Mattis (1911-84) recalled riding the bus from East Windsor to Crane Community School in winter and being asked by the driver to get out and push when it came to a particularly steep hill. Out of the driver's view, kids instead clung to the rear of the bus and dragged their feet in hopes of preventing its climb to the top. (*Windsor Historical Commission collection*)

The Berkshire Street Railway operated buses [J] on Pittsfield routes such as this one in 1955. Today's Berkshire Regional Transit Authority began operation in 1974. (*Berkshire Eagle collection*)

Roadside restaurants catered to a newly mobile public. The Havasnak Kitchen [K] was on the Mohawk Trail near the summit. (*Berkshire Eagle collection, Arthur Palme photo*) The Miss Pittsfield Diner [L] had a booming trade among truckers and tourists, according to Joseph A. Amerio of Pittsfield, whose folks Peter M. (d. 1991) and Lena M. Amerio (d. 1980) took over the eatery on Route 20 in 1936. "After the Turnpike opened in the 1950s, it cut business," Amerio said. (*Courtesy Joseph Amerio*) Emma Decker operated a hot dog stand on Undermountain Road in Sheffield [M] in the 1920s. (*Berkshire Eagle collection, C.S. Hayward photo*)

Oscar S. Hutchinson (1844-1936), veteran station master at New Lenox, built aptly named Lenox trucks **[A]** in about 1917. Hutchinson used the vehicles to haul materials from the depot up the mountain for the construction of the Farnham dam on October Mountain in Washington. (*Berkshire Eagle collection, courtesy Oscar Hutchinson*)

Frank Howard (d. 1940) and John G. Morrow opened an agricultural supply store in Pittsfield in 1903, Howard assuming sole ownership seven years later. The merchant specialized in seeds, farm implements, dairy and poultry items, tools, cutlery, cement and lime. The store was located first on North Street, then moved to Fenn Street. During a transitional period, both horse-drawn and motorized delivery vehicles are seen near the store **[B]**. (*Berkshire County Historical Society collection*)

Trucks

A syndicate organized the Pittsfield Milk Exchange in 1920. Drivers for the dairy, including Roland Archambault (1900-1959) at the wheel of this delivery vehicle in 1924 [C], supplied Delicia ice cream to grocery stores and drugstore soda fountains. The business in 1940 retired its last horses, Silver, Dan and John, and switched to all-motorized delivery. (Courtesy Leonard Archambault family)

Mohawk Beverages, established in 1919 on Tyler Street, Pittsfield, supplied soft drinks to area stores [D]. Founding partners included James J. Canning, who was president until his death in 1948. After repeal of Prohibition, the company became a distributor for alcoholic beverages as well. It took on the Pepsi-Cola franchise in 1935. (*Berkshire Eagle, 1939*)

Gerry Guilds opened a stable and freight business in Pittsfield which, after his retirement in the 1870s, was taken over by his son Frank G. Guilds (1851-1910). It grew to house some fifty horses, forty wagons and trucks at its quarters on Appleton Avenue and to employ nearly sixty men. Its first motorized vehicle was an Autocar [E]. (*Dalton Historical Commission*)

William P. (d. 1917) and Joseph H. (d. 1926)—the Wood Brothers—opened a music store on West Street in Pittsfield in 1880, eventually moving to North Street. Absorbed into another business, Lennox & Fletcher, the store relocated to the Allendale shopping center in 1986. The store was the first in the city to have a delivery truck [F]—a locally manufactured Berkshire. (*Berkshire County Historical Society*)

D

C

E

F

Mohawk Trail

The Mohawk Trail—the modern, paved highway version of the Native American woodland path—opened in October 1914. It has been improved several times since, including in 1939, when an 8,000-foot frost wall was constructed along one section **[A]**. (*Berkshire Eagle collection*)

Charles R. Canedy (1885-1927), far right **[B]**, started the highway's tourism industry with a small wooden stand in 1915 (*Berkshire Eagle collection, courtesy Lewis Canedy*)

The Canedy family operated gift shops and view towers both at Whitcomb Summit and at Hairpin Turn **[C]** until 1980. (*Berkshire Eagle collection, courtesy Ed Longevin*)

A pamphlet touts the Mohawk Trail as the "Scenic Gateway to New England." **[D]** (*Author's collection*)

Rails

The Hudson & Berkshire Railroad, chartered in New York state in 1828, was the first to lay tracks to Berkshire County's border. A 2.75-mile puppet line chartered in 1831 and built in 1838 connected State Line to West Stockbridge village and was Berkshire's first railroad. The first railroad mishap was in West Stockbridge that very year when an engine pulling a train of cars out of the switching yard struck a cow. There were no casualties, however, when this train **[A]** derailed at Merrill Road in Pittsfield in August 1984. (*Joel Librizzi/Berkshire Eagle*)

Bill Russell was engineer and Dennis Cronin was conductor and brakeman on General Electric's industrial switcher engine at the Morningside Plant in the late 1920s **[B]**. Cronin (1866-1947) retired in 1931, according to his granddaughter, Marion E. Hamilton. Hamilton's husband, Thomas M., an engineer in the same yard, is seen in 1967 **[C]** on GE's new Engine 8, along with Jeremiah J. Parker, conductor, and Edward A. Clapper Sr., brakeman. (*Photo and General Electric News for 8 December 1967, courtesy Marion E. Hamilton*)

Berkshire's railroad engineering marvel is the 4.75-mile Hoosac Tunnel between North Adams and Florida, built for the Troy & Greenfield Railroad. It was completed in 1873 after two decades of labor. One mis-start was the purchase of Wilson's Patented Stone-Cutting Machine in 1852. Expected to gnaw a 24-foot shaft into the mountain, it quit after 10 feet, leaving a gash at the eastern portal which is still to be found [D]. (*Berkshire Eagle collection*)

An inspection crew rides a gas-powered car along local lines near the Hoosac Tunnel, 1940s [E]. (*Berkshire Eagle collection, Arthur Palme photo*)

An eastbound train on the Boston & Albany track steams through Hinsdale in about 1930 [F]. The B&A was successor to the Western Railroad, which was chartered in 1833 and first ran in 1841. (*Courtesy Doug and Nicole Pierce*)

Fred Clement, station master and telegraph operator, is among those in front of the new railroad station in Richmond in 1909 [G]. The old station is in the rear. (*Berkshire Eagle collection, courtesy David Dalzell*)

Companion photos in *The Berkshire Eagle's* files carry the briefest of captions. One **[H]** is identified as "The old flagman at Becket crossing of the Boston & Albany Rail Road. Porter Loveland, his wife killed there." Harriet Loveland, 67, died at about 6:30 the morning of April 28, 1906, while on her way to work at a village factory. There were two trains approaching the crossing. She stepped back to avoid one, but was struck by the second and killed instantly. Whether her husband was on duty at the time, or not, isn't stated. But he certainly must have been devastated. The caption on the second photo **[I]** reads, "The new flagman at Becket crossing of the Boston and Albany Rail Road." (*Berkshire Eagle Collection*)

Berkshire's first horse-drawn trolley carried passengers in open cars up West Street from Pittsfield depot to Pontoosuc Lake beginning in 1886. The Hoosac Valley Street Railway between North Adams and Adams was chartered the same year. It ran its first electrified cars in 1889. The Pittsfield Street Railway organized in 1887, electrifying in 1892. Its successor was the Berkshire Street Railway, which in 1901 began construction of a 55-mile line from Adams to Sheffield. The first trolleys in Pittsfield, having served their purpose, are on their way to the scrap yard **[J]**. (*Berkshire Eagle collection, courtesy Henry Robarge*)

Conductor and brakeman pose with a street railway car at the end of the line at Peck's in Pittsfield, circa 1915 **[K]**. (*Berkshire Eagle collection*)

Flight

Pittsfield's stable air currents made it an ideal ballooning center in the early 1900s. The scene **[A]** is probably one of several long-distance races that took off from a site off East Street. (*Arthur Olsen collection, courtesy Judy Foss*)

This is possibly a November 1906 race **[B]** between Cortlandt Field Bishop, who drove a Panhard auto, and J.C. McCoy and Alan Hawley, who piloted the balloon *L'Orient*. Bishop won the prize, driving virtually beneath the airborne craft all the way to North Adams. (*Berkshire Eagle collection*)

H. Roscoe Brinton (1886-1980) with his partner Lowell R. Bayles was the first manager of the Pittsfield Airport on Barker Road. Brinton was an avid competitor in air shows. He also instructed fledgling pilots and flew mail routes. At Pittsfield Airport **[C]** during a Twentieth Anniversary of Air Mail event in 1938, he signs a receipt for Matthew D. Guiltinan, foreman at Pittsfield Post Office. The photographer at right is Irving Sisson of *The Berkshire Eagle's* staff. In a feeder system constituting the first official air mail flights in Berkshire, Ted White flew letters from Canaan, Conn., to Great Barrington, where James F. Tracy added them to his bundle and flew them to Pittsfield to hand over to Brinton. Leonard C. Glover flew in letters collected in Dalton, likewise Sumner Knight came from North Adams. Brinton flew the lot—mostly souvenir cachets for members of the Berkshire Stamp Club—to Westfield. The letters came back to the senders in the next day's mail. (*Berkshire Eagle collection*)

Ted White was field manager for the Brinton-Bayles Flying Service in Pittsfield, and also worked at other airports in the area. Among his students was Lena H. Nott, the first woman to solo from the air field in June 1931. White, an avid parachutist, is seen **[D]** at New Lebanon's air field. (*Berkshire Eagle collection*)

Lowell R. Bayles (1900-1931) **[E]**, co-manager with Roscoe Brinton of the Pittsfield Airport when it opened in 1931, was drawn to speed racing. He piloted the bullet-shaped Granville Brothers' Model Z Super Sportster to victory in the National Air Races in 1931. Bayles died when his plane crashed in an attempt to secure the land plane speed record that December. (*Aero Digest*/author's collection)

Stephanie D. Wilson, **[F]**, who graduated from Taconic High School in 1984, is a National Aeronautics and Space Administration astronaut awaiting her first flight. Story Musgrave, who grew up in the Glendale section of Stockbridge, first flew on the NASA space shuttle *Challenger* in April 1983. He made his sixth flight in 1996, becoming the oldest astronaut (at age sixty-one) until John Glenn's return to space in 1998. Musgrave is seen **[G]** in a 1987 photo. (*Both Berkshire Eagle collection, courtesy NASA*)

Firefighting

Pittsfield, which created a fire district in 1844, has the oldest municipal fire engine company in the United States. Henry Hurlburt [A], a member of Pittsfield's George Y. Learned Engine Co., wears a typical 19th century fire fighter's dress. (*Berkshire Eagle collection, Edman photo*)

Lane Farnum [B], outfitted in modern protective garb, is among Egremont firemen responding to a mutual aid call to Great Barrington in January 1985—on a cold, wintry night—to contain a fire in the Farshaw's store on Main Street. (*Susan Plageman/Berkshire Eagle*)

Fire and water do mix. Silver Lake in Pittsfield ignited in December 1923 [C]. Oil on the water's surface was touched off by sparks from a bonfire on shore. The resulting three-alarm fire threatened the W.E. Tillotson Manufacturing plant and the old "beehive" tenement nearby. The city owned a single chemical truck—and it became stuck in mud on Fourth Street. One fireman stepped on a broken live wire and received a 4,800-volt shock, but was not seriously hurt. Wind eventually drove the fire away from shore and it burned itself out. (*Berkshire Eagle collection, Charles A. Fairfield photo*)

Fire in March 1956 destroyed Shadowbrook in Stockbridge. The 100-room mansion, built by millionaire banker Anson Phelps Stokes (1838-1913), at the time of the fire was a Jesuit novitiate. Perhaps the only photographer to take color slides of the fire [D], in which four died, was Pittsfield's Will Plouffe. (*Courtesy Will Plouffe*)

Legendary Lawmen

It wasn't his biggest case, but it was his most famous. Stockbridge Police Chief William J. Obanhein (1924-94) **[A]** in November 1965 took eighteen-year-old Arlo Guthrie and a companion to Lee District Court, charging them with illegal disposal of rubbish on Thanksgiving. Obanhein said he hoped the youths found the cleanup more work than the littering. Guthrie turned the incident into a popular song, "Alice's Restaurant Massacree." For a motion picture version two years later, Obanhein and Guthrie played themselves.

Pittsfield's Police Chief John L. Sullivan (1882-1943), wearing Badge No. 1 **[B]**, escorts a group of school children across the street. A native of South Lee, Sullivan joined the Pittsfield force in 1909 as a reserve patrolman, working his way up to the chief's position in 1915. Sullivan was one of three police chiefs nationally invited to confer with FBI Director J. Edgar Hoover on the creation of a national training academy. During Sullivan's tenure, a new brick station was constructed on Allen Street and "dirty" magazines were swept from the newsstands.

Charles L. Frink (1849-1937) **[C]** persevered where federal marshals failed—he subpoenaed Standard Oil tycoon John D. Rockefeller Sr. in the 1907 trust-busting case in which Judge Kenesaw Mountain Landis ultimately fined the oil company $29 million. Rockefeller was hiding out at Taconic Farm, the Onota Lake estate (now site of Hillcrest Hospital) his son-in-law and daughter, Mr. and Mrs. E. Parmalee Prentice, were renting for the summer. Frink walked onto the grounds without challenge, approached the main house, found Rockefeller relaxing on the veranda, served the papers, exchanged a few pleasantries and left. A furniture painter in North Adams by trade, Frink later served a term as mayor and by the time he died had worn a badge for five decades. (*All Berkshire Eagle*)

Political Men

Charles H. Warner (1891-1954) **[A]**, Sheffield tax collector, collected the entire levy due each of the forty-eight years he held the job, not a penny less. "I have always tried to impress upon those reluctant to pay that they will have to settle with the town sometime, or their property will be sold...," Warner explained in 1945. "One farmer said he had no money but he did have cows and would I take a couple of them for the tax? I did...." Upon his retirement, he was given a gold railroad pocket watch. (*Berkshire Eagle, C.S. Hayward photo, 1931*)

Hancock Selectmen sign articles at a 1944 town hearing permitting horse and dog racing—if the Massachusetts Racing Commission agreed **[B]**. From left are Attorney Thomas D. Lavelle; Selectman John D. Whitman, promoters John H. Gilbody and James Gillis; Selectmen Harry Sharp and Henry Blain and, standing in the right rear, promoter Donald B. Hughes. (*Berkshire Eagle collection, Gravelle Pictorial News*)

Week-long Boys' State (and companion Girls' State) summer seminars sponsored by the American Legion have explained the intricacies of the American governmental system to thousands of young people. Dr. William J. O'Hearn (1890-1980), a Pittsfield dentist, calls the roll for a group headed to the University of Massachusetts at Amherst in 1941: Earl Suitor of Hinsdale and Kirk Bussiere, Richard King, Gerald Binder, Spencer Smith, Joseph Handler and Thomas Wallace, all of Pittsfield **[C]**. (*Berkshire Eagle*)

Harvey E. Lake (1902-64) meets with John F. Kennedy (1917-63), who is campaigning for a seat in the U.S. Senate **[D]**, in May 1956. A 39-year veteran of General Electric, Lake was elected Pittsfield mayor for one term in 1955-57. He later was a lay pastor for the Windsor Congregational Church. (*William Tague/Berkshire Eagle*)

Political Women

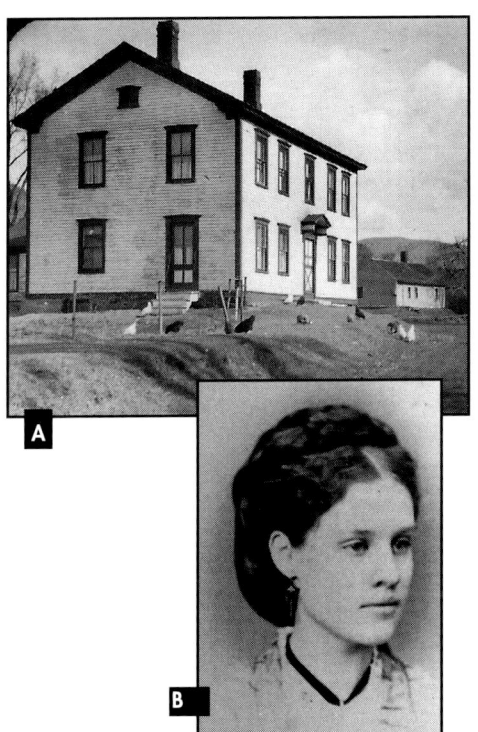

Berkshire women have not shied from standing up for what they believe in. Susan B. Anthony (1820-1906), Adams-born temperance advocate, abolitionist and promoter of women's suffrage, is the first woman to appear both on a postage stamp and on an American dollar coin. Anthony and Elizabeth Cady Stanton organized the National Woman Suffrage Association in 1869 and Anthony traveled, spoke and wrote tirelessly for women's causes. She was arrested in 1872 and charged with illegally voting in an election; she never paid her $100 fine. Her birthsite still stands in Adams **[A]**. (*Adams Historical Society*)

Anthony's counterpart was Anna L. Dawes (1851-1938), a staunch opponent of women's suffrage despite her own long-standing interest in politics and public affairs. Until 1919, Dawes was vice president of the Massachusetts Anti-Suffrage Society and frequently spoke at public meetings. The North Adams-born daughter of Congressman and later Senator Henry Laurens Dawes (he served in Washington from 1857 to 1892), Anna Dawes was once kissed on the cheek by President Abraham Lincoln. The circa 1871 portrait **[B]** was taken by Brady Galleries. The Dawes family later settled in Pittsfield and Anna, a newspaper correspondent for the *Springfield Republican*, was a founder of the Wednesday Morning Club in 1879. (*Berkshire Athenaeum collection, thanks to Katharine Westwood*)

Phoebe S. Jordan (1864-1940) beginning in 1920 was the first person—man or woman—in the United States to cast a ballot in four Presidential elections. Her name was the first read from the list at New Ashford Town Hall and her ballot was first deposited in the ballot box, generally at 5:45 a.m., when polls opened. From 1916 to '32, Hancock led the country in announcing its vote for President. (That distinction has since gone to a town in New Hampshire.) When women secured the vote in 1920 under the Nineteenth Amendment, Jordan, a Republican in politics, walked about 2.5 miles from the family farm to vote. In addition to the farm, Jordan, who never weighed more than 100 pounds, operated a charcoal kiln, one of the last in the county. She personally delivered the product to customers in Pittsfield. She is riding a mowing machine in the picture **[C]**. (*Berkshire Eagle collection, C.S. Hayward photo*)

Margaret Brennan-Gibson **[D]** of Stockbridge, a professor at Harvard Medical School and a member of the Austen Fox Riggs Center staff, served a six-day jail sentence in Nevada in 1988 for participating in a demonstration against nuclear weapons testing in the desert. (*Joel Librizzi/Berkshire Eagle*)

Berkshire County Commission

Looking very distinguished, the Berkshire County Commission at a February meeting in 1939 is absent two regular members, Chairman Frederick H. Purches and Robert S. Tillotson. To conduct business, two associates were drafted to sit in. From left are Associate James W. Punderson (1859-1941) of Stockbridge, a steward at the Red Lion Inn for nearly sixty years; John Henderson (1869-1953), a native of Scotland who lived in Clarksburg and was overseer at Strong & Hewitt Woolen; and Associate Leland P. Jenks (1877-1949) of Williamstown, owner of the Cameron Agency. The office of associate commissioner was abolished just about the time this picture was taken. Legislation calls for Berkshire County government itself to cease as of July 1, 2000, after 239 years. (*Berkshire Eagle*)

Border Flirts

What, you might ask, is a "border flirt"? The best explanation is by example. Levi Beebe (1817-1900) **[A]**, sawyer and surprisingly accurate weather prophet, on one occasion disagreed with politics in Lee. He owned several thousand acres of wooded land (now Beartown State Forest), including another dwelling up the road in Great Barrington. So he relocated there until that town's antics so disgusted him, he moved back to Lee. (*Picturesque Berkshire*)

Allen Davis (1819-1912) **[B]** had a house which straddled the Savoy and Windsor town line. The house sat atop large logs and, the story goes, when the tax levy in one town became onerous, Davis "rolled" the house over to the other for a more favorable rate. (*Savoy Historical Commission, thanks to Jane Benedict Phinney*)

One-armed Jeremiah "Jerry" Swan (1827-1910) **[C]** owned a floating pavilion on Pontoosuc Lake, from which he dispensed liquor—without benefit of license. He usually did business on the Lanesboro end of the lake. But if authorities there were applying too much heat, he simply towed the raft to the Pittsfield side. The whole enterprise came to an end in 1893 when police in both towns combined to shut it down. (*Berkshire Eagle collection*)

Edith A. Markham (1878-1960) **[D]**, and a neighbor, Ruth A. Brigham, in winter 1928 petitioned the Massachusetts Legislature to transfer their homes from Sandisfield to Otis—that is, to move the town boundary. Their reasons had largely to do with social orientation and convenience. Mrs. Markham had previously lived in Lee. But as a Sandisfield resident, she had to take up legal issues in Great Barrington. If she were an Otis resident, she could go to Lee for court and other business. Voters in Otis and Sandisfield were agreeable to a border change, but the state found it frivolous and refused the petition. (*Berkshire Eagle collection, C.S. Hayward photo*)

The Legislature did agree to another boundary shift. The Rev. Thomas S. Hanrahan (1905-77) **[E]** of Housatonic's Corpus Christi Church was active on the town's zoning committee in 1957, raising the ire of Lucille Crissey (1904-87), a zealous opponent of regulation. Crissey complained—rightly, as it turned out—that Hanrahan had no business in town affairs, as the rectory was actually over the line in Stockbridge. Hanrahan, who said he registered as a Great Barrington voter in good faith, moved to another dwelling in the village while waiting out a six-month residency requirement. Town meetings in Great Barrington and Stockbridge voted that 1.75 acres of church land be moved from Stockbridge to Great Barrington, and the new boundary became official in 1958. (*Berkshire Eagle*)

Health Care

The House of Mercy Hospital, established in Pittsfield in 1875, takes its children's ward outdoors for sun and air in 1906 in a donated tent [A], which had previously gone on camping trips to the Adirondacks. The hospital became Pittsfield General in 1949. (*Berkshire Eagle collection*)

A temporary isolation hospital in Sheffield [B] contains an outbreak of smallpox in 1902. Charles Little (1878-1907), the lone patient, was cared for by his mother, Clara Forbes Little, in a hastily constructed building near the Housatonic River. Little survived. The town later burned the building. (*Berkshire Eagle collection, courtesy Caroll H. Mead*)

Dr. Charles H. Richardson (1869-1935) [C] was founder of Hillcrest Surgical Hospital in Pittsfield in 1908 and served as its head from 1911-35. A renowned surgeon, he stimulated the development of a cancer clinic in the city. (*Berkshire Eagle collection*)

Surgeons perform an operation at Berkshire Medical Center in 1982 [D]. BMC was created in 1967 with the merger of Pittsfield General and St. Luke's Hospitals. (*Berkshire Eagle*)

Red Cross opened a civilian blood donor service at the Berkshire Museum in July 1946 [E], collecting 79 pints. Arthur Breed of Stockbridge gives his sixth pint; Mrs. Roy Crosier of Pittsfield, a Red Cross nurse's aid, her eleventh; and Fred C. Nagleschmidt of Pittsfield, a local VFW commander, his first. (*Will Plouffe/Berkshire Eagle*)

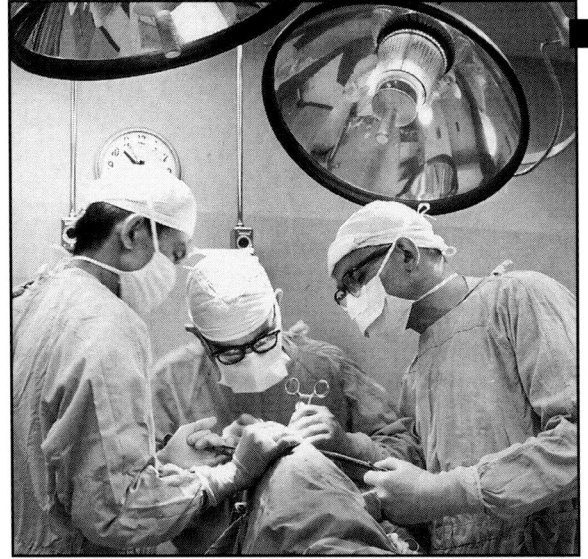

Williams College

Williams College was established in 1790 through a bequest by Ephraim William Jr. (1715-55). A surveyor and military leader at Fort Massachusetts, Williams died at Lake George during the French and Indian Wars. Ebenezer Fitch was the first president of the school, from 1793-1815. Stockbridge-born Mark Hopkins (1802-77) served as president from 1836-72. An inspiring figure, Hopkins initiated radical teaching methods encouraging personal development. Hopkins (seated center) **[A]** is with members of the faculty in 1866, from left: Arthur Perry, John Tatlock and Albert Hopkins; rear, Paul Chadbourne, John Bascom, Charles Treat, John L. Phillips, J.G. Davenport and Franklin Carter. (*Williamsiana Collection*)

Students are totally oblivious to the camera during "Chapel Rush" in 1873 **[B]**. Members of Kappa Alpha, classes of 1869, '70, '71 and '72 fraternity at Williams, pose for the lens in 1868 **[C]**. (*Both Berkshire Eagle collection*)

An oilette postcard circa 1907 **[D]** depicts a rah-rah college spirit. (*Williamsiana Collection*)

RAY-RAY-RAY-
WIL-YUMS-YAMS-YUMS!
WIL-YUMS!

Schools

Sarah V.R. MacDonald (1880-1952) taught in Richmond public schools for five decades. Known as a compassionate teacher, she also tutored Italian workers at Richmond Furnace to speak English and to read and write [A]. (*Berkshire Eagle collection, courtesy Mrs. John V. Boyle*)

School children hold out their hands for cleanliness examination, possibly at Sheffield Center School, about 1900 [B]. A Sheffield teacher and her charges pause for a picture [C]. (*Both Sheffield Historical Society collection*)

Miss Van Horn of Blackinton is the teacher of this fourth grade at Freeman School on Hospital Avenue in North Adams in 1935 [D]. (*Courtesy Donald G. Bishop*)

Barrington School for Girls was active from 1923-48 at Searles Castle in Great Barrington. Students for several years performed a Gilbert and Sullivan operetta in a joint production with Lenox School **[E]**. Proceeds in 1941, typically, went toward purchase of a mobile field kitchen for Great Britain. (*Great Barrington Historical Society, Marie Tassone collection*)

Pittsfield High School students do research at the school library **[F]**. The building on East Street opened in 1931. (*Berkshire Eagle*)

A student completes a drafting assignment at Taconic High School in Pittsfield **[G]**. The facility opened on Valentine Road in 1969. (*Joel Librizzi/Berkshire Eagle, 1988*)

Estates

Members of the Berkshire social set enjoy a tennis party at Wheatleigh in Stockbridge in 1911 **[A]**. Millionaire banker Henry H. Cook built the thirty-three-room mansion in 1894 as a gift for his daughter Georgie (1865-1946), who married Spanish Count Carlos M. de Heredia. Modeled after a sixteenth-century Florentine villa, it is a resort today. Philip Barber (1903-81) and Stephanie Barber converted the carriage barn into the Music Inn in 1950 and offered folk, jazz and pop concerts there for nearly three decades. (*Berkshire Eagle collection*)

Cooking staff prepare a meal in the kitchen at Bonnie Brier Farm in Interlaken **[B]** – an estate built in 1892 by Leonard Forbes, chief engineer for New York City Telephone—in this circa 1893 view. The estate was later owned by Dan R. Hanna, and was site of the first Berkshire Symphonic Festival concerts in 1934. Hans K. Maeder purchased the property and turned it into Stockbridge School in 1948. Today it is DeSisto School. (*Lenox Library collection, Edwin Hale Lincoln photo*)

Marjorie L. Field (1911-97) **[C]**, riding her hunter at the Lenox horse show in 1923, was the daughter of Mr. and Mrs. William B. Osgood Field of Lenox. She married Helm George Wilde (1908-98) in 1932. The Wildes became master breeders of Jersey cattle at their High Lawn Farm in Lee.

Theresa Higginson **[D]**, daughter of Mr. and Mrs. George Higginson of Chicago, took first prize with her mount Larkspur in lady's saddle and hurdle classes at the Lenox horse show in '23. She later married Count Gighlio Rucellai of Florence.

Beatrice Bend Bishop (1902-93) **[E]**, daughter of Mr. and Mrs. Cortlandt Field Bishop of Lenox and New York, rides her thoroughbred hunter in October Mountain State Forest. Bishop attended the Sorbonne and earned her medical degree. She married Adolf Augustus Berle Jr. (1895-1971), a longtime professor at Columbia University and a member of Franklin Delano Roosevelt's administration. (*All Berkshire Eagle collection, C.S. Hayward photos*)

Electrical magnate George Westinghouse (1846-1914) constructed Erskine Park in Lenox **[F]** in 1887 for his wife Marguerite. It was razed in 1919 so a new owner could build Holmwood. (*Lenox Library Association, Edwin Hale Lincoln photo*)

Art collector Grenville Lindall Winthrop (1864-1943), a descendant of John Winthrop, the first governor of Massachusetts, acquired Groton Place in Lenox in 1902. The country manor was built in 1855 by William Ellery Sedgwick, grandson of Theodore Sedgwick, and was one of the earliest "cottages" in Berkshire. Winthrop renovated buildings and grounds and won the Massachusetts Horticultural Society's gold medal for the topiary garden in 1935. Winthrop was a member of the law firm Ludlow, Philips & Winthrop and from 1915-41 was president of the Woman's Hospital in New York. Winthrop was mortified in 1924 when one of his daughters, Kate, eloped with the electrician who helped build the chicken house, and another, Emily, eloped with the chauffeur. Pictured is the library of Groton Place in 1940 [G]. Four years later the property became home to Windsor Mountain School, a preparatory school which closed in 1975. (*Berkshire Eagle collection, C.S. Hayward photo*)

Giraud Foster (1851-1945), inventor of clothing snaps and successor to the family's mercantile business in New York, celebrates his ninety-third birthday [H]. Foster was one of the early and leading figures in the Lenox summer colony and his mansion Bellefontaine was based on Le Petit Trianon, Marie Antoinette's chateau at Versailles. The mansion was one of the last great cottages in Lenox and cost $1 million to build. Yet it sold for only $70,000 at auction in 1946. Today it is home to Canyon Ranch. (*Berkshire Eagle collection*) Young Giraud Vann Nest Foster [I], only son of Giraud Foster, poses with a family pet. The nanny is hiding behind the statue. (*Courtesy Lenox Library Association*)

Rooms

Let's peep in a few windows. Twenty settlers lived in crude Fort Massachusetts and held off as long as they could against Indian attack in 1746. The fortification was located in North Adams near the Williamstown line. Pictured **[A]** is the interior of a replica (now also gone) as it looked at its dedication in 1933. (*Berkshire Eagle collection, Gravelle photo*)

Colonial simplicity is evident in the interior of the Mission House in Stockbridge **[B]**, a dwelling John Sergeant (1710-49) constructed for his bride Abigail Williams in 1739. A property of the Trustees of Reservations, it is maintained as a house museum today. (*Berkshire Eagle collection, Samuel Chamberlain photo*)

More than a century later, furnishings had improved in comfort and style, as witness Henry Ivison's front room in Stockbridge in the late 1870s **[C]**. (*Berkshire Eagle collection, courtesy Mrs. George W. Bartini*)

A college dormitory room without a stereo or personal computer? Well, this students' quarters at Williams College **[D]** was photographed in the late 1880s, after all. (*Berkshire Eagle collection*)

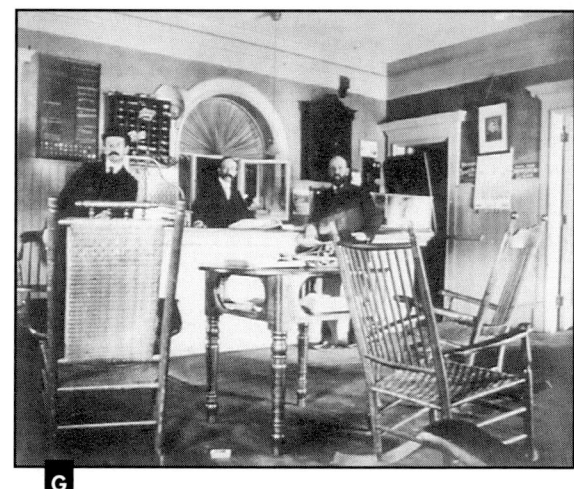

Robert W. Browning of Dalton strums his banjo in the parlor, some time in the 1890s **[E]**. (*Berkshire Eagle collection*)

Anna G. Clement, superintendent of the House of Mercy Hospital in Pittsfield from 1884-1909 and also director of the Pittsfield Training School for Nurses, maintains her office in this room **[F]**. (*Berkshire Eagle collection, courtesy Pittsfield General Hospital*)

The office staff is ready to register guests at the Irving House in Dalton, circa 1900 **[G]**. The establishment was built by papermakers Zenas Crane Jr. (1840-1917) and his brother W. Murray Crane (1853-1920) and named for author Washington Irving (remember one of his characters was Ichabod Crane?). It opened in 1889. After a fire in 1894, it was rebuilt. It became the Crane Inn in 1953, but was torn down in 1966 and is the site of a bank branch office today. (*Berkshire Eagle, courtesy Robert N. Barstow*)

A wood stove in the center of the room testifies to the coldness of classes some winter days at the North School in Mount Washington in 1901 **[H]**. (*Berkshire Eagle collection, courtesy Elizabeth Spurr*)

Wanted posters decorate the wall of the Pittsfield police station in this 1929 picture **[I]**. (*Berkshire Eagle collection*)

Centuryhurst on Main Street Sheffield, built in 1800, by the time Dr. Byron V. Tompkins (1854-1926) and his family bought it a century later was outfitted with modern plumbing **[J]**. (*Sheffield Historical Society collection, Carrie Smith Lorraine photo*)

Architect Joseph McArthur Vance (1868-1948) of Pittsfield retained a rustic atmosphere when he converted a former horse barn into the Wyantenuck Country Club in Great Barrington in 1913 **[K]**. (*Berkshire Eagle collection*)

Another conversion is Nina Larry Duryea's home **[L]**, which was once Allen Sykes Yale's 1810 grist and sawmill in Stockbridge. Duryea (1868-1951), founder of the Duryea War Relief effort during World War I, was an author, inventor and prominent summer resident. (*Berkshire Eagle collection, C.S. Hayward photo*).

The Aspinwall Hotel (also a Vance design) begins serving meals in 1902 **[M]**. The 400-room hotel, which commanded a broad view from Lenox, burned in 1931 and the site today is Kennedy Park. (*Berkshire Eagle collection*)

Pittsfield Housing Authority's Wilson Park housing project off Wahconah Street **[N]** showcases its first homes in October 1948; this is a modern kitchen-dining room of the post-World War II era. (*Berkshire Eagle*)

A pooch relaxes on a sofa in the Dickens Erickson house in Williamstown in 1964 **[O]**. (*Joel Librizzi/Berkshire Eagle*)

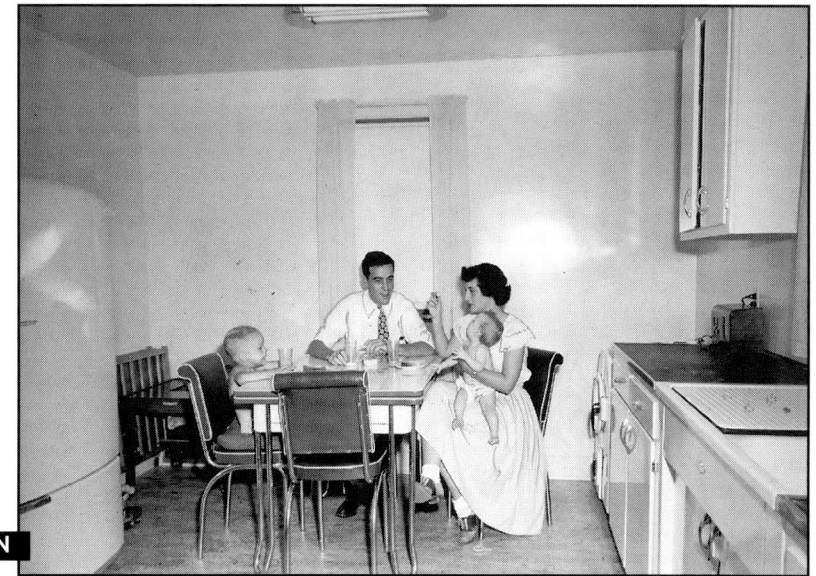

Construction

A construction crew takes time out from erecting a large building in Pittsfield **[A]**. That's no doubt the mustached foreman standing staunchly at center. (*Berkshire Eagle collection, S.S. Wheeler photo*)

The former Berkshire Life building at the corner of North and West Streets in Pittsfield was constructed with four stories and a French mansard-style roof in 1868. The roof was altered in 1911 and raised to a fifth story, as pictured **[B]**. An annex was erected at the west end in 1925. Tenants over the years included the city post office (1868-1911), telephone company (until the 1950s) and several banks. The Masonic Lodge met on the fourth floor until it opened its own lodge on South Street. (*Berkshire Eagle collection*)

Affordable Housing

The first dwellings in Berkshire were by necessity "affordable," as settlers had little means and many responsibilities. A bicentennial recreation of a 1753 colonial home in Williamstown **[A]**—built using period tools and materials—commemorates the town's bicentennial. Joyce Orell, a senior at Williamstown High School, offers a twentieth century contrast in 1953. (*Berkshire Eagle collection, Segar Photographic Services*)

Kelly Houses **[B]** in the Allendale section of Pittsfield are one answer to a post-World War II housing shortage. John J. Kelly of Arlington erected more than 100 homes in 1946, over loud cries from the public that they were made of green lumber and that so many new homes would severely tax water and sewer services. The homes all eventually sold in the $6,500 to $8,000 range. (*Berkshire Eagle*)

Pittsfield contractor Peter G. Francese (1897-1978) **[C]** held the Lustron franchise in Berkshire County and erected more than a dozen of the economical (some sold for $7,800), factory-made, all-metal homes. The first one went up in 1949 on South Mountain Road. (*Berkshire Eagle, 1968*)

Displaying Yankee thrift, Berkshire residents frequently move buildings rather than tear them down. Hancock's 130-year-old Town Hall **[A]**, for example, constructed from materials recycled from an old Baptist church, served as a meeting place, school and library. It is being transported about a half mile in 1975. (*Joel Librizzi/ Berkshire Eagle*)

Funeral home director Milton Stevens relocates the former Fassett home on Elm Street, Great Barrington, to South Street in 1964 **[B]**, temporarily closing Main Street to traffic. (*Great Barrington Historical Society, Marie Tassone collection*)

Moving Buildings

English-born John P. Reddy (1883-1960) was a bricklayer for thirty years before becoming Pittsfield's building inspector in 1948 and superintendent of public buildings a year later. A caption with this picture **[A]** suggests Reddy was supporting a bulge at (then) City Hall—not a serious enough problem to warrant demolition, as the building is still in use today as a branch bank. (*Berkshire Eagle collection, Clay Perry photo*)

A Greek Revival structure built in 1845 in Williamstown as a Methodist church became Waterman & Moore's Opera House. It offered a range of performers on its stage, from Ralph Waldo Emerson (1865) to Groucho Marx (1925). But it was razed in 1992 **[B]**—over public protest—to make room for a Williams College studio art building and parking lot. (*Berkshire Eagle*)

This building on East Hoosac Street in Adams **[C]**, upended by a flood in 1901, became of little use other than as a play structure for neighborhood kids. (*Adams Historical Society, thanks to Eugene F. Michalenko*)

Fire in the Bush and Kennedy Blocks on Pittsfield's North Street in 1979 endangered the Pittsfield National Bank and other neighboring buildings. The remains of the structures were removed **[D]**—unplanned urban renewal. (*Courtesy Leonard Archambault*)

Razing Buildings

Hotels

Berkshire's hospitality trade began to thrive after the Civil War. Theodore Roosevelt (1858-1919) pauses in front of Heaton Hall, Prospect Hill, Stockbridge **[A]**. The hotel was designed by architect W. Edward Weeks of Pittsfield in 1903 for Congressman Allen T. Treadway, whose family owned the Red Lion Inn. A posh resort in its day, its guests included presidents, ambassadors and prominent musicians. It was razed in 1972 and Heaton Court is on the site today. (*Berkshire Eagle collection, courtesy Mrs. Alden Wellington*)

After an earlier hotel at the corner of Main and Holden Streets in North Adams burned, sewing machine inventor and manufacturer Allen B. Wilson (1942-88) purchased the land and in 1866 built the four-story brick Wilson House **[B]** at a cost of $140,000. (*Berkshire Eagle collection, courtesy Anthony Marino*)

William T. Staples **[C]**, a doorman at the Wendell Hotel in Pittsfield, in 1939 examines new Amelia Earhart luggage made in Parkwood, Texas, using General Electric plastics. Samuel Bowerman (d. 1952) built the Wendell at the corner of South and West Streets in 1898, naming it for Col. Jacob Wendell, a prominent figure in Pittsfield history. The posh hotel was twice enlarged, but fell to the pressures of urban renewal. It was leveled in 1965 to make way for the Berkshire Common. (*Berkshire Eagle*)

Jane Fitzpatrick **[D]** of Stockbridge with her husband, former Sen. John H. "Jack" Fitzpatrick, established Country Curtains in 1956, nurturing it into a major manufacturing, mail-order and retail operation. The Fitzpatricks in 1968 bought the Red Lion Inn in Stockbridge, and in 1980 Blantyre in Lenox. (*Berkshire Eagle collection, Sydney M. Kantor photo*)

The aerial view of Park Square in Pittsfield [E] shows the old Wendell Hotel—by this time the Hotel Sheraton—and front-in parking on North Street. Fires and urban renewal have changed the picture considerably today, particularly in the areas of McKay Street and West Street, on the left. Park Square (which is actually oval) was site for many years of the Old Pittsfield Elm, which stood 126 feet tall. One celebrated attempt to down the tree in 1775 was thwarted, thanks to the pleadings of Lucretia Williams. Her husband John donated a parcel of land large enough for a village green around the tree and Pittsfield gave land from its own holdings to create the park. The tree succumbed to lightning in 1864, at age 340. (*Berkshire Eagle collection, Gene Mitchell photo*)

McKinley Square in Adams looked like this in 1940 **[A]**. The William McKinley statue was erected through the efforts of industrialist William Plunkett, a longtime presidential friend, and was unveiled in October 1903, two years after the chief executive was assassinated. (*Berkshire Eagle*)

Trolleys were in their heyday when this scene was snapped **[B]**, probably before 1910, on North Adams' main thoroughfare. (*Berkshire Eagle collection, courtesy Lewis Canedy*)

Lee's venerable Morgan House is at the center in this view of Main Street **[C]**. The inn was built as a private residence circa 1817 by William Potter and became a stagecoach inn in 1853 under the ownership of Edwin Morgan (1812-85). Among those signing the guest book over the years were Horace Greeley, "Buffalo Bill" Cody and U.S. Grant. (*Berkshire Eagle collection, courtesy Lee Library*)

Great Barrington's Housatonic village **[D]** had grown so by the early 1900s, Monument Mills physically moved dozens of mill houses and established a new street. (*Berkshire Eagle collection, Fred Sauer photo*)

Streetscapes

James H. Barnes and his family drive along State Road in Richmond in 1907 **[E]**. Barnes (1873-1969), known as "Mr. Telephone," with his cousin Jesse Fairfield earned a share in the fledgling Richmond Telephone Company in 1903 by pledging a stand of chestnut trees which was cut down for poles. In 1923, Barnes became general manager of the company, and later president. Barnes and his wife, the former Martha Peirson (d. 1966), had three daughters. (*Berkshire Eagle collection, Matthew Morrison photo courtesy David Donald*)

Hartsville village's profile, in about 1900 **[F]**, includes a church which was later converted into a grange hall and is privately owned today. (*Frank E. Sisson collection, courtesy Linda Thorpe*)

The general store on Route 9 in Windsor **[G]** is now in the third generation of Estes. Jerome A. Estes (1850-1931) established the business in about 1880. His great-nephew Ralph I. Estes then carried on the business, succeeded by W. Henry Estes (1909-89) in 1939. After Henry and his wife Helen C. Estes (1913-89), who was Windsor postmaster for thirty-four years, retired in 1970, their son Kenneth C. Estes became proprietor. (*Berkshire Eagle collection*)

Dwight M. Maynard's Dalton

There were Maynards in Dalton beginning in colonial days. In a later generation, William D. Maynard (1828-1903) gave up the farm on Day Mountain to settle in a house on Main Street. Son Dwight M. Maynard (1858-1914), a bachelor, worked as a master mechanic at various times for E.D. Jones & Sons and Stanley Electric, both of Pittsfield, and Spark Coil Co. of Dalton. He was also a toolmaker for General Electric.

An avid amateur photographer, Dwight Maynard often took his nephews Harold D. Maynard (1888-1965) and Theodore Pomeroy (1883-1969) with him on picture-taking excursions around the town. That's probably Harold Maynard on the stump on then-clear-cut Day Mountain in about 1895 **[A]**, the village visible in the background. This book's front cover shows Grandfather William Maynard, grandson Theodore Pomeroy and son Dwight Maynard reading in the parlor in 1898. Dwight's niece Margaret Maynard (1899-94) **[B]**, with her pet rooster, graduated from Dalton High School and Berkshire Business College and worked in the Crane & Co. office from 1910 until she retired in 1954. (*All Maynard collection, courtesy Raymond W. Fischer*)

More views from the Maynard camera: A diesel locomotive chugs up the grade from Pittsfield into Dalton [C], passing Crane & Co.'s Old Berkshire Mill; a power transformer in assembly [D] overshadows the three men at the Stanley plant in Pittsfield in about 1906; Millury Shaw Maynard [E] sits by a brook in East Windsor while on a picnic outing (she married Harold Maynard, nephew of the photographer); and Millury's father Jesse Shaw [F], proprietor of a small store in East Windsor, makes deliveries by wagon.

Frank E. Sisson's Mill River

Jedediah Sisson (1773-1854) apprenticed at a sawmill on the Konkapot River in Mill River, and eventually acquired the business in 1857, and was succeeded by his son Henry Sisson (1812-95) and grandson Henry Dwight Sisson (1836-1914). The latter also held public offices in town, county and state government. Henry Dwight's son Frank E. Sisson (1872-1943?)—an amateur photographer—continued the mill, making shingles, cheese boxes and paper pulp until closing at about the time of World War I. Frank's brother Harry Dwight Sisson (1863-1938) took the family trade to Pittsfield in 1883 when he established a box factory which he later sold to the Eaton-Hurlbut Paper Company. He then started a Buick auto dealership. He served in several municipal capacities and was mayor from 1903-04. (His son Irving was a *Berkshire Eagle* photographer.)

Frank's wife Mary Rhoades Sisson bore two daughters, Rachel (who would grow up to marry George Aakjar) and Eleanor (who would wed Dr. Robert Sellew), but died during a third childbirth. Frank re-married and moved to Springfield, where he worked as a mechanic for a Pierce-Arrow and Buick franchise until he retired.

These scenes have been newly printed from original dry plate negatives. In the group photo [A] are all Sissons: front from left, Rachel, Frank's oldest daughter; Harry, William and Irving, Frank's nephews; middle row, Mary, Frank's wife; Emily P. (Spaulding) (1835-1923), Frank's mother; Elizabeth (Welles) (1861-1955), Frank's sister-in-law; Nellie, Frank's sister; and Harry Dwight, Frank's brother; and rear, Henry Dwight, Frank's father, and Sarah, Frank's aunt.

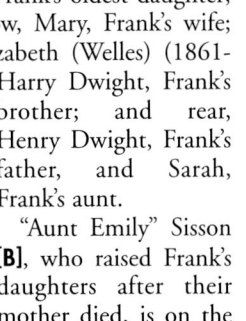

"Aunt Emily" Sisson [B], who raised Frank's daughters after their mother died, is on the porch with a family pet, the same dog that shows up in a photo with Rachel [C]. Frank and Mary are in the yard with young Elinor [D]. (*All Frank E. Sisson collection, courtesy Linda Thorpe, with an assist on identifications from John Sisson*)

A wide range of subjects caught Frank Sisson's eye, including venerable Eugene Howe [E]; scholars and their teacher at New Marlborough Central School [F]; an unidentified group of hunters [G]; and the Sisson sawmill [H].

Carrie Smith Lorraine's Sheffield

Carrie Smith Lorraine (1868-1935) was a semi-professional photographer who snapped pictures of one and all at her family's Orchard Shade rooming house on Maple Avenue in Sheffield. Lorraine's mother, Eliza Hubbell Smith (1842-1915), started Orchard Shade in 1888 and it was still in the family a century later. In the photo [A] are, from left, Carrie's father Maloy John Smith (1834-1910), a paperhanger by profession; Carrie's sister Dora Smith Mead (1882-1965) and Carrie, both of whom also took turns operating the inn; and third sister Eliza.

Gilbert (or perhaps Robert) Smith, nephew of Carrie, plays with pet cats [B] while Dora and a guest [C] perch in one of the trees which gave the boarding place its name. Neighborhood girls visiting Orchard Shade in about 1895 [D] are Agnes Montague and Salli Tompkins. (*All Carrie Smith Lorraine collection, Sheffield Historical Society's Mark Dewey Research Center, thanks to James Miller*)

Carrie Smith Lorraine took pictures of neighbors including Edward Augustus Croselar (1831-1915) **[E]**, a member of the all-black Massachusetts Fifty-Fourth Regiment during the Civil War. In later years, back home in Sheffield, Croselar was active in the Grand Army of the Republic fraternal organization. The veteran was born in New York state, while his wife, Lucy A. (1850-1905), was a Sheffield native.

All but one of these children **[F]** is from the town's black community. Charlie Williams takes a wagon full of Orchard Shade guests for a hay ride, circa 1900 **[G]**, with a noticeably gaunt horse. Juli Tompkins **[H]**, wife of a physician, adjusts her watch in the bedroom of her home Centuryhurst on Main Street. (*Wagon photo Berkshire Eagle collection, courtesy Carroll H. Mead; others from Sheffield Historical Society collection*)

G

H

E

F

Hancock Shakers

Members of the United Society of Believers in Christ's Second Appearing lived frugally, simply and chastely. Followers of the religious teachings of Ann Lee (1736-84), Shakers, as they are popularly known, established a village at Hancock, west of Pittsfield, in 1790 and it remained active for 170 years. Today as a museum of Shaker history, its buildings include the 1826 Round Stone Barn, the 1830 communal Brick Dwelling and eighteen other restored structures. A car leaves a trail of dust in the panoramic view **[A]**, circa 1915, which shows the Church Family complex including several buildings such as the large white Sisters' Shop on the left which no longer exist.

Nellie L. Cameron (1906-85) was the only person to teach at the Shaker Village's North School who was not a member of the sect. She was a Baptist. Born in Hancock, she began teaching at the Village in 1928, and remained at her desk for thirty years. She wrote the bicentennial edition of *Hancock Through the Years* in 1976. Cameron is seen with Geraldine Moore **[B]**, a Shaker child, in 1937; at the time Moore was the only student in the school. The Boston *Sunday Post* noted that spring, "8-Year-Old Girl Wins Every Honor in Her School." (*Courtesy Hancock Shaker Village*)

Brother Ricardo Belden (1868-1958) **[C]** was the last male member of the Hancock community. Orphaned at age four, Belden was placed in the care of Shakers at Enfield, Conn. He showed an early talent for mending broken machinery, and in later years repaired wooden clock works. After that colony closed in 1917, he worked in "the world" for a decade then came to Hancock in 1927. (*All courtesy Hancock Shaker Village, thanks to Sharon Duane Koomler*)

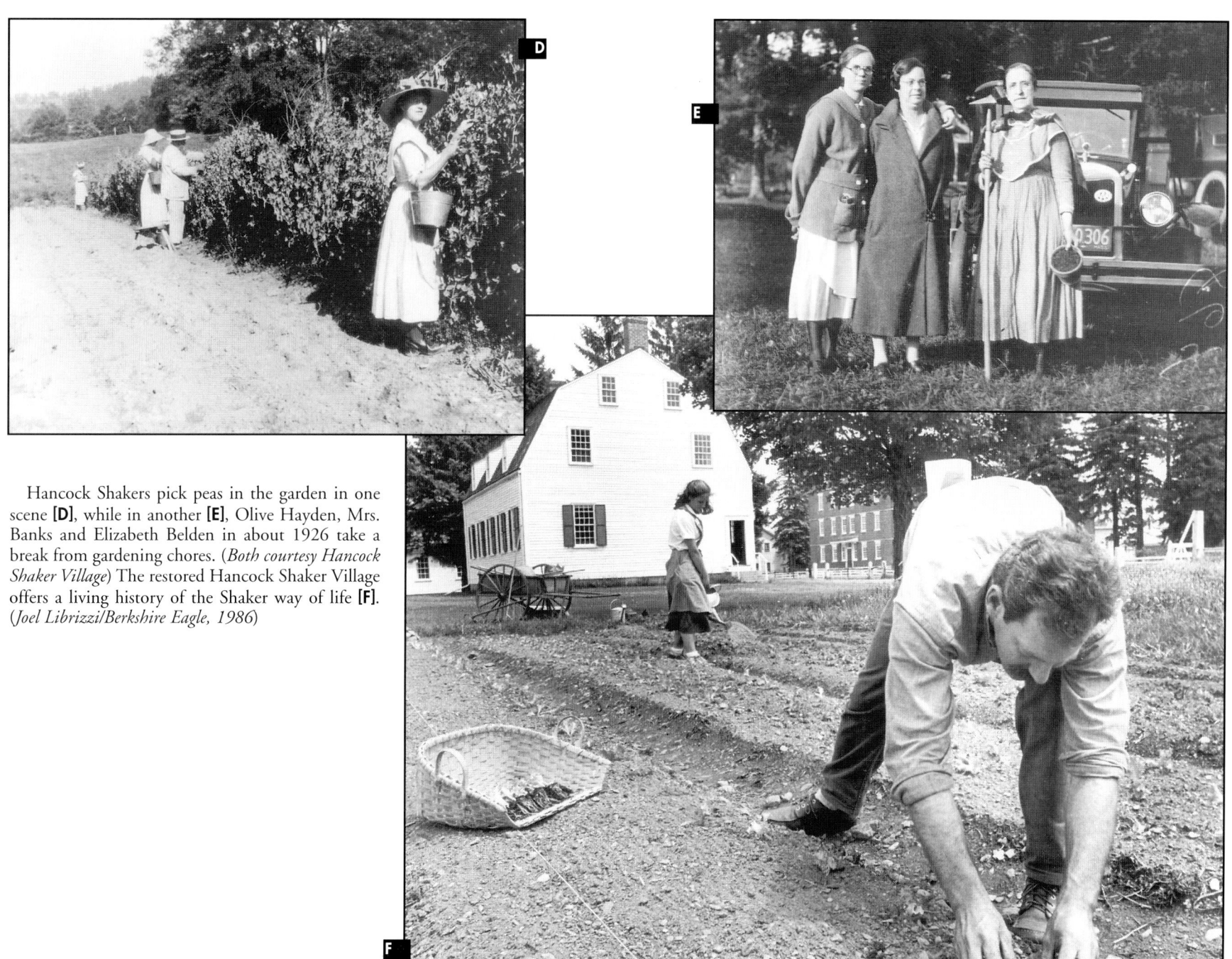

Hancock Shakers pick peas in the garden in one scene [D], while in another [E], Olive Hayden, Mrs. Banks and Elizabeth Belden in about 1926 take a break from gardening chores. (*Both courtesy Hancock Shaker Village*) The restored Hancock Shaker Village offers a living history of the Shaker way of life [F]. (*Joel Librizzi/Berkshire Eagle, 1986*)

Retailers

"Mayor" Frank Creamer (1862-1930) **[A]**, proprietor of a country store in Peru, was a Democrat long active in town politics. He at one time held thirteen offices. When regulations forced him to resign as postmaster after twenty-seven years, his wife Bertha took the appointment. One newspaper reporter described Creamer's store as "more like a curiosity shop. It was Mr. Creamer's proud declaration on many occasions that his store contained anything that a customer desired. Everything from pins and needles to a mahogany pulpit could be bought there...." The store building is now part of Johnsonville Village in East Haddam, Conn. (*Berkshire Eagle collection, C.S. Hayward photo*)

Thomas Norton (1847-1935) **[B]** grew up in Williamsville and was a foreman at Rockdale Mills. In 1872 he moved to Lee and started a bakery, from which goods were peddled by wagon, and opened Norton House on Main Street. He vowed to never sell alcohol or do business on Sunday, and in April 1918, when Prohibition began, he reportedly "went out and ran up his flag" in celebration. (*Lee Library collection*)

Herbert R. Messenger (1871-1946) operated a plumbing, hardware and tinsmithing business in the Central Block in Dalton **[C]**. Retailing was in the family; his son Charles (1899-1992), returning from the service, in partnership with his father opened a Ford agency which was active from 1922-68. (*Dalton Historical Commission*)

Deborah A. Donovan opened her first Cottage store in Sharon, Conn., in 1969, selling a mix of housewares, gifts and clothing. **[D]** Cottage eventually expanded to six outlets, four of them in Berkshire County. Donovan, who served as president of the Berkshire Hils Conference, eventually sold the shops and became an interior and graphic designer. A Pittsfield store, which opened in 1975, was closed in '98 by successor owner Linda P. O'Connell. Stores in Lenox and Stockbridge are now gone, but Williamstown Cottage is still doing business. (*Alan Cooperman/Berkshire Eagle*)

Henry E. Tiedemann (1871-1940) and family operated a bakery business on Summer Street in Adams, selling groceries, confectioneries, cigars and fancy goods. Tiedemann, who came here from Buffalo, N.Y., ran the business for two decades, then became associated with Adams Baking. He was also president of Adams Cooperative Coal Co. Tiedemann's daughter Florence R. Tiedemann (1901-90) is shown **[A]** with her Aunt Clara Heinig Malloy inside the store. Clara's sister (and Henry's wife) Helen and Florence's sisters Hazel (d. 1985) and Mildred (d. 1979) at times helped out in the sales room. Henry Tiedemann, at right in another view **[B]**, readies a delivery cart to make the rounds. The man with his arms crossed is not identified, but he shows up in a second, studio photo **[C]**, posing proudly with one of his baked goods. (*All Adams Historical Society, thanks to Eugene F. Michalenko*)

Tiedemann's Bakery

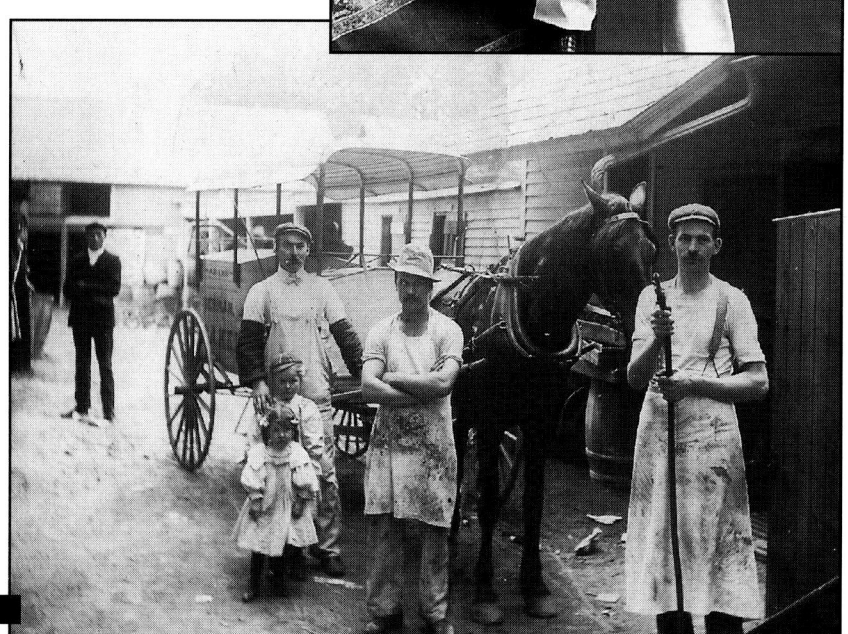

Grocers

Paul (1884-1973) and Apolonia Gwozdz Trzepacz (d. 1963) opened a store on Wahconah Street in Pittsfield in 1914. A native of Poland, Trzepacz worked from time to time as a court interpreter. This store scene from 1920 [A] shows Apolonia and Paul, and Apolonia's brother. In front are children Walter and Stephen (seated on a cracker box), Edward and Wanda. Pork and beef hang in the window. The large box by the door holds eggs. The three sons later succeeded to the business—which sold Royal Scarlet brand groceries—until the chain stores cut too severely into business and they had to close, according to Edward's widow, Mary Trzepacz of Pittsfield. "It was long hours, six days a week, short pay, no insurance, no retirement," she said. The store was well known for its kielbasa. "They would come from miles to buy it. There was no filler (dried milk or cereal). The meat was smoked with apple wood. We sold three or four tons at Easter." (*Courtesy Mary Trzepacz*)

Jacob Wineberg (1895-1989) fled Czarist Russia at the age of eighteen, coming to Adams in 1915. Working in an uncle's store for $5 a week, Wineberg managed in two years to save enough to start his own business, which he called the Adams Cut-Rate Market. With his son Mervin (1918-79), Wineberg developed a seven-outlet, countywide, multi-million dollar operation. Grandson Howard J. Wineberg later headed the family business, which was sold to Big Y Foods of Springfield in 1984. Jacob and Mervin Wineberg are pictured with Edward Ginsberg at the opening of the first Adams Supermarket in Adams in 1948 [B]. (*Adams Historical Society, thanks to Eugene F. Michalenko*)

Eating

Bridge Lunch owner Tommy O'Laughlin purchased a new custom diner made by the Jerry O'Mahoney Co. of New Jersey in 1924 and installed it at the corner of Eagle and North Streets in Pittsfield **[A]**. "We used two gross of eggs each day," recalled Thomas Avalle (1906-96), who as a teenager helped at the grill. "I'd arrive at work at 4 a.m. to help the German baker Reipert make donuts. They had to be ready for when it opened at 6." (*Berkshire Eagle collection, Gravelle Pictorial News, 1933*)

Serving dishes are heaped high at Jug End Barn in 1960 **[B]**. The popular Egremont resort reached its heyday in the 1950s and '60s under the management of Angus and Mimi Logan MacDonald. Most of the buildings are gone and the 3,000-acre property since 1994 has been owned jointly by Department of Environmental Management and Department of Fisheries & Wildlife. (*Warren D. Fowler/Berkshire Eagle*)

Everyone has one of these pictures in their photo album **[C]**. Louis Esterman (1905-81) and his wife Ella Rosenblum Esterman (1904-89) of Pittsfield are surprised with a fifteenth wedding anniversary party by friends and relatives in 1940. The Brooklyn, N.Y., natives—he was a General Electric toolmaker, she was a sales clerk at England Brothers—had one son and one daughter. They went on to observe their gold and emerald anniversaries. (*Berkshire Eagle collection*)

Men enjoy good food and companionship at the Raja deer camp in Becket in 1938 **[D]**. (*Berkshire Eagle collection, courtesy Oscar Hutchinson*)

One can almost smell the aroma at the Italian booth **[E]**, which has its kitchen outdoors at the August 1976 Ethnic Fair in Pittsfield (*Berkshire Eagle*)

The food court at the Berkshire Mall in Lanesboro **[F]** is full of lunchers as soon as it opens in 1988. (*Susan Plageman/Berkshire Eagle*)

79

"I shall never forget that first Thanksgiving dinner," recalled Agnes Gould (1870-1958), describing one of the first meals held at Gould Farm. She and her husband Will Gould (1873-1925) established their home-style therapeutic community in Monterey in 1913—an endeavor which, in other hands, thrives to this day. "Our feast consisted of a few vegetables, which made us think of the verse from the Book of Proverbs, 'Better is a dinner of herbs where love is, than a stalled ox and hatred therewith.'" Will Gould is at left center; his wife smiles across the table from him **[A]**. (*Gould Farm collection, thanks to Kim Hines*)

John A. Howden (1909-1997) **[B]** developed two well-known varieties of pumpkin—the perfect filling for a Thanksgiving pie—the Howden pumpkin and the Howden "Biggie." Harris Seed still markets the seeds. Born in Penang Straight Settlement, off the coast of Malaysia, where his father worked for a British shipping company, Howden came to the United States as an infant. After attending agricultural school, he eventually acquired a farm in Ashley Falls. (*Seth Lipsky/Berkshire Eagle, 1966*)

Leland M. Stone talked turkey. The Washington farmer **[C]** raised upwards of 500 birds of Mammoth Bronze and White Holland stock for Thanksgiving tables. "Yes, sir, I'm the only mother those birds ever knew," he declared in 1929. The former Maine woods guide also raised blooded rabbits, game pheasants, White Leghorn hens and swarms of Italian bees. (*Berkshire Eagle collection, C.S. Hayward photo*)

Thanksgiving

Clambake in Stockbridge

Edward L. Pilling (1896-1954), Stockbridge fire chief for more than twenty years, loved to put on clambakes. Typically, the volunteer fire department hosted a cookout at the Dan Hanna Farm (now DeSisto School) in 1936 for about fifty firemen and their friends from neighboring Lee. That's the chief, on the right, enjoying corn on the cob **[A]**. Cooks check their steaming clams and corn **[B]**. After-meal entertainment includes dancing **[C & D]**—to a bagpiper!—and a softball game. Among guests is Allen T. Treadway (1867-1947) **[E]**. Born at, and later owner of, the Stockbridge (now Red Lion) Inn, Treadway was first elected to Congress in 1913 and spent 33 years in office.

The pictures are by professional photographer David Milton Jones (1867-1946), a welfare worker and inspector of tenement houses in New York before coming to the Interlaken section of Stockbridge in 1912 to become superintendent of St. Helen's Fresh Air Home. (*Stockbridge Library Association Historical Collection, thanks to Barbara Allen*)

England Brothers

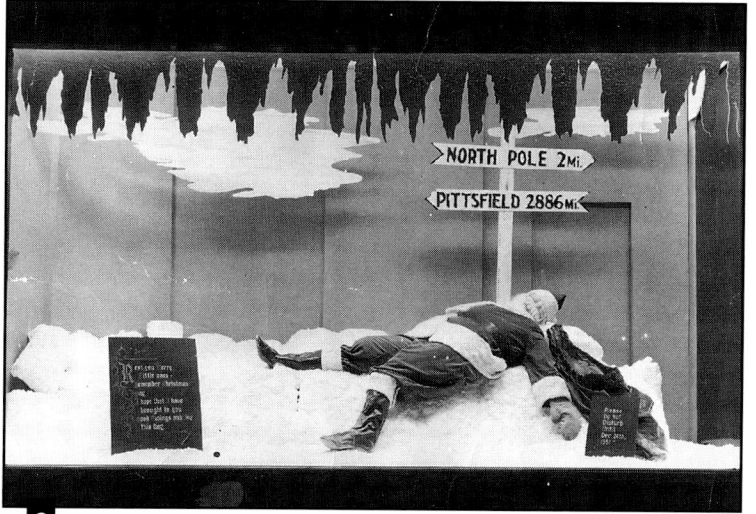

England Brothers' escalator [F] was one of the first installed in this country. (*Will Plouffe photo, courtesy Andrew Blau*)

Exhausted after a busy holiday season in 1950, a snoring Santa Claus [G] takes a break in the England Brothers display window. (*Courtesy Andrew Blau*)

It is wall-to-wall people but they seem to be enjoying their shopping excursion in April 1956 [H]. (*Warren D. Fowler photo, courtesy Andrew Blau*)

Pittsfield's beloved department store started out as a dry goods mercantile run by brothers Moses and Louis England in 1857 in the former Burbank Block [A]. Moses England's sons Benjamin and Simon in 1886 entered the business, as did their brother Daniel in 1891, the year it moved just south of the Newman Block at the corner of North and Depot Streets [B]. In 1904 England Brothers expanded into the entire four-story building and in 1911 took over half of the Newman Block, adding two stories to the building in 1925 and '26 [C]. By 1931, the store occupied that entire block, and increased the height to create a uniform building [D]. The third generation of Englands, Daniel Jr., Simon Jr., Benjamin H. II and Alan Blau (husband of Rose England) entered the business. Satellite stores opened in Allendale in 1969 and in North Adams in 1976, the same year Andrew J. Blau, great-grandson of Moses England, became president. The North Street store's last facade, of composition material, was installed in 1966 [E & back cover]. The 130-year-old business, one of the rare family-owned department stores to operate for that length of time, closed in February 1988. After attempts to find new uses for the building, it was razed in 1998 to make way for a new City Savings Bank. (*All courtesy Andrew Blau*)

Moses England (1830-98) **[I]** was born in Germany and came to Pittsfield by way of Albany, N.Y. (*Courtesy Andrew Blau*)

An England Brothers bookkeeper **[J]** smiles from her desk in about 1900. (*Berkshire Eagle collection, courtesy Ralph W. Hutchinson*)

England Brothers routinely entertained or honored longtime employees. Sales clerks enjoy an outing at Camp Merrill on Pontoosuc Lake, Pittsfield, in 1926 **[K]**, during the flapper era. (*Berkshire Eagle collection*) Members of the Century Club attend a dinner in 1949 at the Wendell Hotel **[L]**. (*Courtesy Andrew Blau*) Employees gather on the lawn at Eastover during a company picnic in June 1958 **[M]**. Eastover is the former Harris Fahnestock estate in Lenox which George Bisacca (d. 1983), a one-time Ringling Brothers roustabout, purchased in 1944 and turned into a resort with a Civil War motif. (*Courtesy Art Marasco*)

Natural Entrepreneurs

Some Berkshire entrepreneurs made a modest living from the environment. An early natural attraction for local residents and visitors was Stevens' Glen in Richmond. Romanzo Stevens (1843-1925) **[A]** and his wife Mary Jane (Root) Howes Stevens (1839-1928) **[B]**—they celebrated their fifty-fifth wedding anniversary in 1925—allowed paid entry to the attractive ravine, which is now owned by Berkshire Natural Resources Council. The Stevenses had a small dance pavilion at the top of the gorge which drew an estimated 900 people to one outing in 1919.

Mail carrier Isaac "Ike" Whitbeck (1862-1924) **[C]** of Mount Washington caught and sold rattlesnakes. His regular clients included Raymond L. Ditmars, reptile curator at the Bronx Zoo. Whitbeck, "king of the rattlesnake handlers," once nabbed as many as fifty slitherers in a single excursion, carting them home in a burlap bag. He holds one of his wriggling reptiles in a homemade set of tongs. Zoologists visiting the Whitbeck home were apt to meet up with Whitbeck's wife Mary **[D]** and any of their nine children. Whitbeck died from a freak accident in Copake, N.Y.; he was thrown from a wagon, fracturing his skull and breaking his neck.

Carey Stillman Hayward (1875-1951) took the photos on this page, and others scattered throughout the book. A newsman for fifty-three years for the *Springfield Republican* and other papers, Hayward had an eye for some of the more intriguing Berkshire residents of the 1930s. (*All Berkshire Eagle collection*)

Coal

Coal carrier Benjamin "Uncle Ben" Wilson (d. 1886) **[A]** worked for Pittsfield freighter Gerry Guilds. According to the legend on this studio card, he was "30 years at 'The Old Stand'" on Depot Street. He poses with the tools of his trade: a shovel and a basket.

Cecil Calvert Gamwell (1854-1941) **[B]**, as evidenced by his clothes and setting, prospered from his coal business. Gamwell opened his dealership in 1877 on Columbus Avenue in Pittsfield. Surviving a disastrous fire in 1908, the firm relocated to the corner of Fourth and Lincoln Streets **[C]**. Gamwell brought his sons Cecil C. Jr. (1892-1947) and Clarence L. (1878-1964) into the company with him and eventually retired in 1935. Clarence ran the business on his own when Cecil Jr. left to raise potatoes. (*All Berkshire County Historical Society collection*)

Pittsfield Coal Gas erected a woodframe gas holder house on Deming Street in 1873, eventually bricking the exterior **[D]**. The tank held gas produced by baking coal in retorts. The gas company eventually built metal holding tanks on East Street (since demolished) and the old gas holder house was used variously for a mattress factory, auto garage and furniture warehouse and office for Berkshire County Association for Retarded Citizens until it was destroyed by fire in 1991. (*Picturesque Berkshire*)

Beer

Bartender Luke Huban (1860-1926) serves up drinks to an after-work crowd at the Eldorado Inn in Lenox Dale in about 1910 **[A]**. Built just after the Civil War, the Eldorado burned in 1967 and a nearby shuffleboard alley was converted into a new barroom. (*Berkshire Eagle collection, courtesy John J. O'Brien and Harold Harris*)

Prohibition erased business of the Berkshire Brewery in Pittsfield **[B]** in 1919. Established on Columbus Avenue in 1866 by Jacob G. Gimlich (1845-1912) and his brother-in-law John W. White (1839-1916), natives of Bavaria and Germany, respectively, it brewed Mannheimer Export Lager, Lenox Half Stock Ale, Greylock Ale and India Pale Ale. Its second plant, built in 1890, yielded 325 barrels a day. (*Berkshire Graphic Supplement, 1894*)

A worker loads the five-barrel Peter Austin brewing system at Old Saddleback Brewing in Pittsfield **[C]**, established in 1994 as part of a local brew pub, The Brewery on Depot Street. Owner Paul A. Fortini made the brewery into a separate business three years later, distributing British-style ales to the local market. (*Courtesy Old Saddleback Brewing*)

Tyringham Rakes

Captain Thomas Stedman was the first of his family to settle in Tyringham. His son William Stedman (1795-1870) started a woodworking shop in the town in 1827 which continued through his son Martin V.B. Stedman (d. 1895) and then his grandson Marshall W. Stedman (1859-1935). Marshall, who took over in 1887, is seen with one of his rakes in about 1930 **[A]**. Marshall had a gift for self-promotion and presented gift rakes to American presidents including Theodore Roosevelt, William Howard Taft and Grover Cleveland. A workman shapes a rake tooth **[B]**, one of about 25,000 shipped annually during the company's heyday. A truck loaded with wooden rakes is ready to leave the factory **[C]**. The structure burned in 1978 and the business, by then in other hands, never reopened. (*All Berkshire County Historical Society collection, Glen S. Cook photos*)

Industry

Berkshire Glass of Lanesboro, one of three glassworks in the county, was active from 1847 to 1901. It made plain, tinted, ribbed and window glass for Tiffany, Crowninshield and other clients. John Carroll (1825-1912) **[A]** is the last surviving worker of the Berkshire enterprise. (*Berkshire Eagle collection*)

Byron M. Hollis [1858-1929] **[B]** of the Bush section of Windsor operates a spruce oil distillery, selling the liquid product in large drums to pharmaceutical companies which used it to make balms for muscle relaxants. Frederick F. Bird (1897-1982), who also made the distillate, recalled, "I got 32 cents a pound, later 35 cents was offered by a man in Savoy, so I sold to him." (*Berkshire Eagle collection*)

Berkshire Coated Paper **[C]**, located on the Housatonic River in Great Barrington, in what was originally the Russell brothers' Berkshire Woolen mill, is menaced by flood waters in 1948. Coated Paper closed in about 1960, according to Bill Arienti, whose father Fermo Arienti worked there until the end. The building was razed in 1968. (*Courtesy Bill Arienti*)

Edwin Dorr Griffin Jones (1824-1904) came to East Lee in 1845 to train as a wheelwright. He moved to Pittsfield in 1866 to start his own business making pumps, wheels, elevators and other equipment for the paper industry. Machine shop employees trim a beater shaft in the photo **[D]**. Doing business internationally, the company was sold to Beloit Iron Works of Wisconsin in 1958. Two years later, a new plant was constructed in Dalton at a cost of $1.8 million. Beloit-Jones in 1998 announced plans to close the local plant. (*Berkshire Eagle collection*)

Iron

Berkshire boasted several iron furnaces in the nineteenth century. The one in Richmond became the largest and lasted the longest. The blast furnace, erected in 1829, was modified over the years. By 1914, production was nearly 12,000 tons of high-grade, close-grained pig iron annually. The wage was $8.40 a week. Angelo Balestro (1911-90) remembered workmen changed their clothes at the end of the day: "They'd wear the same work clothes all week, wash them at the end of the week." A view of the works [A] shows the furnace at left, the office at right. (*Berkshire Eagle collection, courtesy Peter Pieklo*)

Charcoal burning in communities within a 25-mile reach of Richmond left the hillsides barren of trees. The scene of an about-to-be-fired kiln in Alford [B] also shows several feminine visitors. (*Berkshire Eagle collection*)

The track out of the Klondike Mine in Richmond is seen in October 1909 [C]. Richard Malumphy (1896-1985) recalled the shaft went down about 125 feet and there were three levels. Miners worked in pairs, using picks and shovels to follow the drifts. Malumphy's brother was one of two men trapped by one underground cave-in. "They got them out in a half hour," Malumphy said. "They knew enough to blow out their candle—it would have taken all of their oxygen." (*Berkshire Eagle collection, courtesy M.H. Hall*)

The furnace shut down after World War I. The remains have been nominated for inclusion on the National Register of Historic Places, according to William F. Edwards of the Richmond Historical Commission.

Stirring some criticism from neighbors, but wowing those who attended, was a private dance production (permission was denied for a public performance) called "Twelve Incantations" by choreographer Laurie McLeod of Stockbridge-based Victory Girl Productions at the furnace site in November 1997. Albany's *Metroland Magazine* called it the "Best Dance of the Year." One of three performers was Bettina Montano, seen in costume on the rock wall [D]. (*Carol Gingles photo, courtesy Laurie McLeod*)

Quarries

Berkshire quarries provided stone for countless local landmarks, and a few national ones. The Briggs quarry in Sheffield, for example, supplied marble for a layer of the Washington Monument in 1879-80. The photo **[A]** shows the cutting shed in 1876. (*Sheffield Historical Society*)

North Adams quarries produced stones for grave markers, mantel pieces, fire jambs and hearthstones. In 1884, masons Charles and Merrill Whitney had a small quarry off Walnut Street **[B]**. (*Berkshire Eagle, courtesy Randy Trabold*)

Duane Northrup began the manufacture of lime in Cheshire in 1847. After the Civil War, he sold the business to Alfred and Albert Farnum, who ran the mines until selling to the Curtin brothers in 1904. This view in the 1940s **[C]** is after Farnam-Cheshire Lime merged with U.S. Gypsum. The business closed down in the 1960s. (*Berkshire Eagle collection, Arthur Palme photo*)

Lee Steam Marble Works was one of the area's most successful family owned and operated businesses, supplying stone for Grant's Tomb in Washington, D.C., St. Patrick's Cathedral and the State House in Boston. The quarry **[D]**, off Marble Street, was started some time before 1850 by Rice, Baird & Heebner. Under a lucrative contract with the federal government in 1852, it furnished about 491,000 feet of marble to enlarge the capitol building in Washington. Francis "Frank" Gross (1836-1902) succeeded his uncle Charles Heebner as quarry foreman, and he and with his brothers Charles H. and William H. continued the business. (*Mason Library*)

Textiles

Textile production, once a major Berkshire industry, is now all but gone. The old Berkshire Mill No. 3 in Adams, for example, was razed in 1969. President William McKinley (1843-1901) had laid the cornerstone of what became the largest factory in the town while visiting his friend, cotton manufacturer William B. Plunkett (1850-1917), in 1899. Charles T. Plunkett (1855-1927) was also associated with his brother in this mill and also Greylock Mills in North Adams. Pictured are employees in the mulespinners room at the Berkshire Mill's Room 4 **[A]**. (*Adams Historical Society, thanks to Eugene F. Michalenko*)

Wyandotte Worsted operated in Pittsfield from 1931-63 (before that it was known as Pontoosuc Woolen Manufacturing) and at one time employed 500 workers **[B]**. (*Berkshire Eagle collection*)

Frank W. (1826-1906) and James H. Hinsdale (1833-1912), descendants of the Rev. Theodore Hinsdale, for whom the town of Hinsdale was named, opened a woolen mill there in 1852. It soon had seventeen sets of cards and sixty-seven broad looms in two stone and one wooden building, now gone. In 1886, the Hinsdale Mills employed about 250 operatives making cassimeres, kerseys, suitings, etc. **[C]** The brothers eventually moved to Pittsfield. Carried on by other hands, the mill in Hinsdale finally closed in 1931. (*Courtesy Joseph Blake family*)

Pittsfield-born Arthur H. Rice (1855-1927) **[A]** graduated from Williams College in 1872 and joined his father William B. Rice, a manufacturer of silk, and S.K. Smith in organizing A.H. Rice Co. at the corner of Robbins Avenue and Linden Street in Pittsfield in 1878. The plant initially employed thirty hands. The Rices bought out Smith and moved the factory to Spring and Burbank Streets in 1886. They enlarged the facility and brought in new equipment including a mohair braider in 1893. Norman Lewis tests parachute cord at the silk mill **[B]**. (*Both Berkshire Eagle collection*)

A.H. Rice Corp., a still-busy maker of thread, braid and knitted specialty products **[C]**, worked behind the scenes on many pioneering projects. It produced special insulation for Admiral Richard E. Byrd's second Antarctic expedition, for example, and braided tape for electrical cables for Apollo moon flights. (*Berkshire County Historical Society collection*) Frank C. Carmel (1893-1961) **[D]** joined A.H. Rice in 1905 as a sweeper and was foreman of nearly every department before becoming superintendent in 1930. Carmel, seen behind his office cage, was active in civic affairs and was twice elected president of Hillcrest Hospital. (*Courtesy A.H. Rice Corp.*)

A.H. Rice

Glendale Dam & Hydro-Electric Plant

Monument Mills in the Great Barrington village of Housatonic evolved from an 1844 cotton twine manufactory into one of the largest and longest lasting textile factories in Berkshire County. During a period of growth, the factory, which produced Marseilles counterpanes (bedspreads), among other items, acquired the former Glendale woolen mill property upstream on the Housatonic River and in 1905-06 constructed a new 277-foot dam and a five-generator hydro-electric plant. The dam was the highest one yet on the river. The power plant was equipped with Stanley equipment made in Pittsfield. It is still generating electricity today, even though the mills closed in 1956.

A steam-powered shovel **[A]** loads dirt into horse-drawn wagons during excavation for the retaining wall and 1,600-foot enclosed canal intended to carry water from the dam downstream to the turbines. Contractor J.R. Lee of Patterson, N.J., at times employed as many as 160 men, 20 mules, eight or nine teams of horses, a power shovel, stone crusher and other machinery during construction of the Glendale flume and power station **[B]**. The dam **[C]** is 31.5 feet thick at the riverbed. It is filled with some 3,000 cubic yards of concrete. *(Ramsdell Library collection, Fred W. Sauer photos)*

General Electric

Once Berkshire's largest employer, General Electric in Pittsfield grew out of Stanley Electric Manufacturing, established in 1890 to produce SKC electric generators. Inventor William Stanley (1858-1916) **[A]** was the first to demonstrate the practical application of the alternating current transformer in Great Barrington in 1886. (*Berkshire County Historical Society collection*)

Stanley and partners established an electrical manufacturing plant on Renne Avenue in Pittsfield, soon moving to Morningside. General Electric acquired the plant in 1903 and quickly expanded. That's a new East Plant under construction in 1945 **[B]**. (*Berkshire Eagle*) The Pittsfield facility specialized in power generators and transformer products until the division closed in 1987, leaving a legacy stained by an ongoing debate and fight to have the company clean PCB-contaminated properties and the Housatonic River. GE sold its Aerospace operations to Martin Marietta in 1992 and subsequent sales of that operation ended with its severe shrinkage in 1998.

To keep its workers informed, the company began publishing *GE Current News - Pittsfield Works* as a monthly in 1913. It went through frequent name changes and in 1934 became a regular newspaper under the name *General Electric Pittsfield Works News* **[C]**. The weekly paper's circulation peaked at 15,000 in the 1940s and in 1948 it won a national award from the International Council of Industrial Editors. It was later called simply *GE Pittsfield News*. Under the name *Aerospace*, it published its last issue in March 1993, when the ordnance division was sold to Martin Marietta. (*General Electric Pittsfield Works News for 7 January 1944, courtesy Joseph Amerio*)

Pittsfield's General Electric was a small city unto its own, employing 13,645 hands at its peak in 1943. The plant from the beginning supported its own fire department. Adams-born Willard E. Crossett (1876-1934), a veteran of the Spanish-American War, headed the Pittsfield Works Patrol and Fire Department from 1918 until his death. The photo **[D]** shows some of the gathering as he is honored in November 1942 after serving twenty-five years as chief. One hundred-fifteen members of the uniformed guard force attend the gathering at the Wendell Hotel.

General Electric at work in 1939: John P. Plankey, assembling a regulator [E]; Anita Condon [F]; unidentified worker [G]; and the welding shop [H]. (*All courtesy of The Berkshire Eagle*)

General Electric employed a corps of engineers at its Pittsfield works, among them Anton B. Olsen (1876-1974). Olsen specialized in lightning research; he receives a company award [I], center, as his son Arthur, right, looks on. Olsen and his wife Martha (1880-1974) were avid cross-country skiers in their homeland, Norway, and they helped introduce the sport to the Berkshires. They imported and sold skis and Olsen gave lessons at the Country Club of Pittsfield and later Berkshire Park in Cheshire.

Anton Olsen was among GE engineers in May 1929 [J] demonstrating for the first time a million volts of man-made lightning, striking an electrical sub-station at Silver Lake. Lightning experiments continued for several years under the direction of Karl B. McEachron (1889-1954), the inventor of Thyrite, a resistance material used in a variety of lightning protection and other electrical applications.

Arthur Olsen followed in his father's footsteps, becoming both a GE engineer—he retired from the distribution protective equipment division as a design engineer in 1971—and skier. Arthur belonged to the YMCA's swimming and gymnastics teams [K]. His wife Virginia Denison Olsen (1908-93), seen in a 1939 photo [L], was also a skier; she worked in the payroll department at GE. The Olsens were members of the Mount Greylock Ski Club, which established Goodell Hollow ski area in Williamstown in the early 1930s. Arthur and his brother Corey J.B. Olsen—who retired in 1968 from GE as a model maker and designer—took their mechanical talents outside the plant. The brothers built and flew their own airplane, powered by a small European car motor, and their own racing car in 1928. And Corey built and swam in his own diving helmet in 1933. (*Arthur Olsen collection, courtesy Judy Foss*)

The earliest patent issued to a Berkshirite was to Levi Brown of Adams in May 1806 for a wagon wheel box. The second local patent went to John Scripture of Alford in December 1807 for a butter churn. Jumping ahead several generations, Daniel W. Fox (1923-1989) **[A]** was a tireless experimenter and the discover of Lexan, a plastic used in everything from automobiles to compact discs. Fox, who held forty-nine patents, came to Pittsfield in 1956. He is seen at the dedication of the GE Plastics Technology Center in Pittsfield in July 1984, examining a specially commissioned sculpture, "Genic Doran Divider," crafted by Thomas J. Patti of Plainfield. (*Joel Librizzi/Berkshire Eagle*)

When stiff competition from national bridge manufacturers wiped out the market for his patented iron pipe highway bridge, East Windsor resident Charles H. Ball (1861-1928) **[B]** purchased a portable sawmill and started a woodworking enterprise. His High Ball Mill produced wooden candy sticks, meat skewers and coat hangers for twenty years. (*Berkshire Eagle collection, C.S. Hayward photo*)

Clarence J. Bousquet (1889-1966) **[C]** came to Pittsfield in 1919, opening a sporting goods store and tire outlet. He purchased a farm on Tamarack Road in 1930 and raised mink and cattle. He began flying in 1920 and over the years owned three airplanes of his own, including the first licensed seaplane in Berkshire County. He sold seventy-five acres of the property to the City of Pittsfield for the present municipal airport. In winter 1931-32, Bousquet took a keen interest in skiing and the slopes on his farm became Bousquet Ski Area. Bousquet is credited with a number of innovations including his patented rope tow grippers and devices for tying nylon fishing leaders. (*Berkshire Eagle*)

Inventors

Paper

Pioneer Berkshire papermaker Elizur Smith (1812-89) **[A]** with partner George Washington Platner (circa 1810-55) established Platner & Smith in Lee in 1835. The company in 1867 produced the first pulpwood paper made in the United States. The wood pulp was processed at a small facility in Interlaken and transported to Lee for manufacture. A successor company, Schweitzer-Mauduit International, is still active in the town. Smith became involved in other ventures, including Smith Paper, which he started in 1866 with nephews Wellington (1841-1910) and DeWitt Smith (1840-1908). The son of a farmer, Elizur Smith established Highlawn Farm (later owned by the Wildes) as a stock farm. (*Lee Library collection*)

Byron Weston (1832-98) before the Civil War worked for Platner & Smith in Lee. Freshly mustered out of the Massachusetts Forty-Ninth, he took charge of the Old Defiance Mill in Dalton for his uncle, Franklin Weston, in 1863. Within four years, Weston was the mill's owner and enjoyed a reputation as a manufacturer of high-grade cotton fiber books, ledgers, index Bristols and other specialty papers. The company has been a subsidiary of Crane & Co. since 1956. Pictured is the inspection room in about 1900 **[B]**. (*Berkshire Eagle collection*)

Henry D. Cone (1836-96) worked as a bookkeeper for the Hurlburt Paper Mill in South Lee, then joined Owen Paper in Housatonic. Through his marriage to the widow of that firm's owner, Cone eventually assumed ownership of the business. Owen Paper made fine quality writing and ledger paper. The machine room is shown circa 1875-80 **[C]**. Cone began construction of a grand new factory building just down stream on the Housatonic River, but died before it was completed. That factory is today home to Rising Paper division of Fox River Paper. (*Berkshire Eagle collection, courtesy Mrs. George W. Bartini*)

Arthur Watson Eaton (1852-1934) came from a Connecticut papermaking company to manage the Hurlbut Paper plant in South Lee in 1883. Seven years later he established a subsidiary business, Hurlbut's Author's Linen, which packaged and marketed fine writing papers to such success the division in 1893 moved to a three-story factory building on South Church Street in Pittsfield which had once housed Eli Terry's clock manufactory. The writing paper enterprise grew and soon purchased the business of Hard & Pike. William A. Pike (d. 1927) **[A]** brought his skills in finance and flat paper manufacture to the company. The firm evolved into Eaton-Hurlbut Paper and acquired Berkshire Typewriter Paper Co. and Sisson & Robinson, box makers, in 1901.

Acquisition of a large stockholding by members of the Dalton Crane family in 1908 resulted in a new name: Eaton, Crane & Pike. Bricks are stacked high in this view from the teens **[B]**, during construction of Building 12 at the Eaton Paper complex. There were later corporate changes through 1967, when Textron of Providence, R.I., bought the company and at the same time acquired W.A. Sheaffer Pen Co. The former merged into the latter in 1976, becoming Sheaffer-Eaton. After the business closed, Clock Tower Associates purchased the complex in 1989, and it has been home to *The Berkshire Eagle* and other major businesses.

A worker operates the wooden ruling machine at Eaton's in 1924 **[C]**. Bessy Grey runs the knife folding machine in another 1924 view **[D]**. Workers don cowboys and Indians garb **[E]** for an employee appreciate day. Lillian Peters of North Adams was among Eaton, Crane & Pike employees beginning in 1929. She began with the company earning 23 cents an hour, according to her employee record **[F]**, quickly working her way up through various positions to assembly. She was forced to take a 5 percent wage reduction in 1932, fell into a group payment system two months later and in 1933 was "not satisfied with working conditions and left of her own accord." (*All Berkshire Eagle collection, thanks to Martin Langeveld*)

Eaton Paper

A

B

C

E

D

F

Idle

Berkshire is an industrious county, but it has not gone without labor strife. In the photo **[A]**, workers walk out against General Electric in Pittsfield in October 1960. The longest strike here was a 101-day walkout ending in February 1970—the seventh major strike against the electrical manufacturer since 1916. (*Joel Librizzi/Berkshire Eagle*)

For those temporarily out of work, Kevin Gregoire's is among familiar faces at the Division of Employment Security office in Pittsfield in 1991 **[B]**. (*Joel Librizzi/Berkshire Eagle*)

When Sprague Electric in North Adams closed in 1985 **[C]**, it ended one of the city's larger manufacturing operations. Robert C. (1901-91) and Julian K. Sprague (1903-60) established an electronics plant in Quincy in 1926, based on the former's design of a radio tone control, or condenser. They moved the business four years later to North Adams, where their father Frank J. Sprague (1857-1934), the "Father of Electric Traction," had gone to school. Robert Sprague, company president from 1925-63, according to one social historian practiced a "welfare capitalism" that kept inspired worker loyalty and kept labor unions at a distance until 1966. The 28-building factory complex, abandoned in 1985 when Sprague Technologies pulled up stakes, is now home to Massachusetts Museum of Contemporary Arts. (*Susan Plageman/Berkshire Eagle*)

Conflict

Berkshirites have participated courageously and honorably in every conflict from the French and Indian Wars to Desert Storm. Col. Henry Knox (1750-1806), a Boston bookseller, joined the militia at the outbreak of the American Revolution. In the winter of '75, he took charge of the transport of cannon and mortar from Fort Ticonderoga south to Albany then east through the Berkshires to Boston to assist in the defense of Dorchester Heights. Eight men and their teams arrived in Egremont and Great Barrington in January 1776, and trekked to Otis and Sandisfield and on to Westfield by the end of the month. John Treadwell, holding the reins, is among participants in a 1976 re-enactment **[A]**. (*Author's collection, Berkshire Courier photo*)

During the Civil War, a slave entered the tent of Capt. (later Col.) Henry H. Richardson (1826-1904) **[B]** one night and begged for help in escaping the enemy. Richardson brought the man back to Pittsfield with him and to the end of his days championed civil rights. Richardson was active in the construction business. His projects included a new Pittsfield high school in 1876. (*Berkshire Eagle collection, courtesy Mrs. A.C. LaBelle*)

Lyman Hathaway, an 18-year-old farmer from Windsor, enlisted in the Massachusetts Forty-ninth Regiment Volunteer Infantry when it formed in October 1862 under the command of Capt. William Francis Bartlett (1840-76). Later promoted to general, Bartlett was Berkshire's highest ranking soldier of the war. After basic training at Camp Briggs in Pittsfield, the Forty-Ninth sailed to Louisiana and took part in a bloody assault on Port Hudson. Hathaway survived the fighting and returned to Pittsfield, mustering out in September 1863. He lived his later years in Savoy and is eighty-seven when this picture **[C]** was taken in 1931. (*Berkshire Eagle collection, C.S. Hayward photo*)

Funeral services are conducted in March 1899 **[D]** at the armory in Adams for three men from Company M, Second Massachusetts Infantry, U.S. Volunteers — Cpl. George E. Whipple and Pvts. Joseph Gravel and David C. Ferguson — who died of typhoid fever in Cuba during the Spanish-American War. (*Adams Historical Society, thanks to Eugene F. Michalenko*)

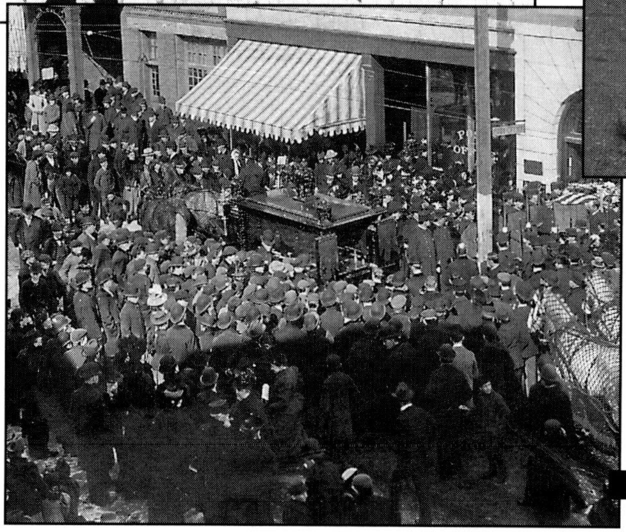

Several Berkshire men served under the command of Major Charles W. Whittlesey (1883-1921), **[E]** a Williams College graduate and Pittsfield resident, in a September 1918 campaign in France's Argonne forest. The 308th Infantry, ordered to advance, became isolated for five days and was severely assaulted by German fire. The "Lost Battalion" refused to surrender, and on the sixth day, American troops relieved what survived of the corps. Whittlesey was awarded the Congressional Medal of Honor. The toll was heavy on Whittlesey. Within three years, the World War I hero was lost at sea while on a trip to Havana, a suspected suicide. (*Berkshire Eagle collection*)

Local men await the posting of draft notices at *The Berkshire Eagle*'s bulletin board on North Street Pittsfield in October 1940 **[F]**. Topping the list are Benjamin Bissell, William F. Mendel, William T. Derivan and William F. Murtagh. As the names are read off, there is a ringing "bingo" from one man in the crowd. (*Berkshire Eagle*)

Returning to Pittsfield on their first weekend leave are early recruits Francis Dwyer, Francis Dow, Edward Shorey, Raymond Callahan, Richard Previtali, William Derivan and James Boland **[G]**. (*Berkshire Eagle collection, Gravelle Pictorial News*)

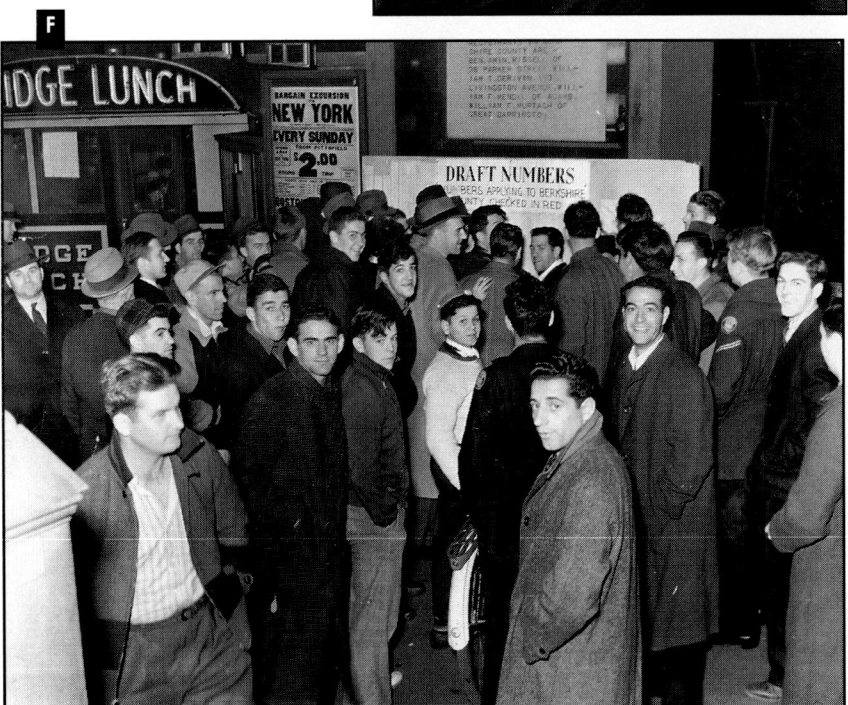

William Delevan sells 110 Newsboy Defense Stamps to Anna Sargeant **[H]**, his first customer, during a campaign in December 1941. Mrs. Sargeant worked at Fred P. Cloutier's office in Pittsfield. Other youths are avid collectors of scrap newspaper **[I]** and aluminum **[J]** during drives in 1941. Their older counterparts include residents of the Berkshire County Home for Aged Women **[K]**, who knit for the Red Cross and British Relief in October 1943. Shown are, from left, Susie Millard, Ida Paine and Mrs. Lane E. Irwin.

Residents mobilize to watch for enemy attack, staffing observation towers such as this one in Hinsdale **[L]** around the clock. Children at Davis School express their feelings about the war **[M]**. (*All Berkshire Eagle*)

Dorothy Luz of Pittsfield **[N]**, a foreman for Elmvale Worsted for nine years, joined the Red Cross Ambulance Corps motor unit and, when the Women's Army Air Corps organized, was the first Berkshire woman to enlist. (*Berkshire Eagle, Gravelle photo*)

V-J Day, Aug. 15, 1945, was a time of great celebration in Pittsfield **[O]**. (*Berkshire Eagle*)

Many Berkshire communities have established memorials to veterans. Canon Robert S.S. Whitman and Jeannette Coakley dedicate a plaque on front of Lenox Town Hall in May 1983 in memory of those who served in the first two World Wars, Korea and Vietnam **[P]**. Whitman served as an Army chaplain in the Philippines during World War II and was rector of Trinity Church from 1949-80. (*Loaned by the photographer, Art Marasco*)

Sports

The Brayton (North Adams) Football Team of 1906 [A] was Berkshire County champion, according to Rita Campbell, whose grandfather Lester C. Jones is in the top row, second from left, and her uncle, Benjamin Jones, is in the bottom row, second from left. (*Courtesy Rita Campbell*)

That's the No. 9 green in the foreground, the No. 5 in the background, as seen from the clubhouse at the Berkshire Hills Golf Course [B]. Eighteen local men formed the club in 1924 when they purchased 120 acres from the old Allen Farm in Pittsfield. Denis T. Noonan (1875-1952), a Berkshire Woolen executive, was the first club president. New York golf course architect A.W. Tillinghast designed the greens. A clubhouse was completed in 1927. (*Berkshire Eagle collection*)

Heavyweight contender Leo Barriere [C], known professionally as "Leo Gates the Mohawk Indian," was the oldest of four boxing Barriere brothers (Lou, Eddie and Bernard were the others) from Adams. Leo fought in the semifinal to the Dempsey-Firpo bout at the Polo Grounds in New York and later became a New York police officer. (*Adams Historical Society, thanks to Eugene F. Michalenko*)

Boxer Dave Shade (1902-83), "Uncrowned King of the Welterweights," twice fought for the world welterweight title, battling Jack Britton to a fifteen-round draw after twice knocking the champion down in February 1922 and losing a controversial decision to Mickey Walker in September 1925. Born in California, Shade in the 1920s had a training camp in Sandisfield, on what is now called Shade Road [D & E]. He later lived in Pittsfield and operated Dave Shade's East Side Cafe from 1934 to '51. (*Courtesy Tom O'Gara*)

A

B

C

D

E

More than a dozen county residents played Major League baseball, and even more have been active in the minors. Thomas Siok (1919-94) **[A]**, a three-sport Searles High School standout in Great Barrington, for example, joined the Kingsport, Tenn., Cherokees in the Class D Appalachian League in the late 1930s and, except for a turn at bat for Uncle Sam, continued his catching career with other teams until 1950, when he hung up his spikes and came home to work for Rising Paper. When his son David Siok coached the Egremont Mets a few years ago, "Skeets" showed up to offer tips to grandson Skye and umpire a few games. (*Courtesy David and Renata Siok*)

Wahconah Park in Pittsfield **[B]**, the 2,000-seat stadium which in recent years has been home to the Pittsfield Mets, was built in 1950 by contractor David McNab Deans of Williamstown. The park, notorious for facing west, over the years hosted such teams as the Hillies and the Electrics. (*Berkshire Eagle collection*)

The Hillies **[C]** of the Class A Eastern League had their greatest moment on Labor Day 1919 when, with the Wahconah Park bleachers jammed with 5,000 people, the team staged an uphill fight with Gary Fortune on the mound to defeat Worcester, 5-3, and grab the pennant. Worcester was ahead 3-0 at the top of the sixth. The Hillies scored two runs in their at-bat, then three more in the seventh to gain the lead. The team dropped out of the league in 1930. Sponsor Philip A. Wilkinson (1887-1951) was proprietor of tobacco stores in Pittsfield and Great Barrington. (*Berkshire Eagle*)

The most lop-sided—and exciting—ball game played in the county was in 1935 when Garrett F. "George" Troy (1884-1944), owner of a Ford auto dealership in West Stockbridge and sponsor of a semi-pro team, lured Connie Mack's Philadelphia Athletics for an exhibition game. Troy Garage's had lost only one game that season, but was still ill-matched against the Phillies, who didn't even bring their star pitcher, Jimmy "Double X" Foxx. The final score was 9-5 in favor of the Phillies. Irving Fenton was among those attending the game—and he came home with his ticket **[D]** autographed by the legendary Athletics manager. (*Courtesy Irving Fenton*)

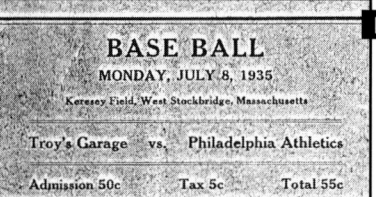

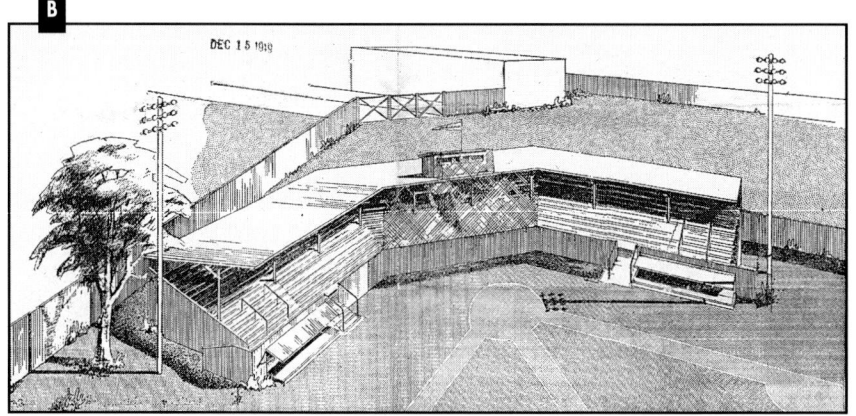

Baseball

Swimming

A sunny summer day draws a large crowd of bathers to City Beach at Pontoosuc Lake in Pittsfield in 1940 **[A]**. (*Berkshire Eagle*)

Sheila Beneat directs the water ballet team which practiced and performed at Eastover Resort in Lenox **[B]**. (*Photo by and courtesy Art Marasco, 1962*)

Bathing suits have required increasingly less material in the years since these were in vogue at Stockbridge Bowl's Tin Can Point in 1913 **[C]**. (*Berkshire Eagle collection, from Lucy C. Brown album*)

Debra Clark and Charles Albert take an unanticipated swim in Stockbridge Bowl during the September 1979 running of the Josh Billings Run-Aground **[D]**. The annual triathlon which began in 1977 includes bicycling, canoeing and running segments. (*Mark Mitchell/Berkshire Eagle*)

The first Pittsfield Ski Club at Berkshire Park in 1910 imported its skis from Norway. Among those pictured **[A]** are Anton Olsen (third from left), Alex Nicholson (fifth), Charles Olsen (tenth) and Andrew Olsen (twelfth). By 1939, there were officially listed some 371 ski runs in Berkshire, four jumps, three tows and one toboggan chute. (*Berkshire Eagle collection, courtesy Mrs. Edward Olsen*)

I.D. Townsend, A.H. Cochran, U. Roland Palmedo and E.S. Spink Jr. are the first Williams College ski relay (cross country) team during the winter of 1916-17 **[B]**. Palmedo organized the Williams carnival and the Williams Outing Club and went on to become the first president of the original Mt. Mansfield development at Stowe, Vt. (*Berkshire Eagle collection*)

Among the region's legendary (and now defunct) slopes is Thunderbolt on the east side of Mount Greylock, a 1.55-mile trail with 2,060 feet descent. It was popular with amateur and collegiate racers. This is the old finish line as it looked in 1936 **[C]**. (*Berkshire Eagle collection*)

Heidi Voelker in 1988 receives a standing ovation at Pittsfield's City Hall after taking second in the U.S. Alpine Championships giant slalom that winter. She represented the United States in the Calgary Olympics **[D]**. (*Bob McDonough/Berkshire Eagle*)

Skiing

Snow Removal

All manner of devices have been used to clear streets and ways. Surely a homemade contraption, this plow is mounted on a tractor to clear the ice [A].

The white fluff is so deep in 1920, it brings Pittsfield's mayor, Louis A. Merchant (1860-1950), out of his city hall office to lend a hand on the sidewalk at the corner of North and West Streets [B]. Merchant was one of the organizers of the Automobile Club of Berkshire County and was for twenty-five years cashier for Berkshire Life Insurance, later opening his own steamship ticket and insurance business.

The Blizzard of 1888 was so severe it derailed this train in West Pittsfield [C].

Several passes with this rugged truck finally opens Benedict Road to Crane Avenue in 1947 [D]. The area experienced a particularly heavy snowfall that February—45 inches in Pittsfield, with precipitation every day for sixteen days straight. (*All Berkshire Eagle collection*)

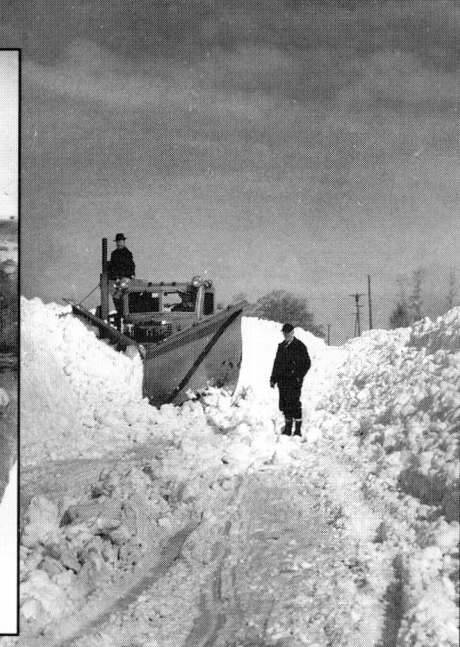

Ice

In the days before refrigeration, ice was harvested from virtually every Berkshire pond. A gasoline-powered saw makes short work of the ice on Pontoosuc Lake, the operators champing on cigars all the while **[A]**. (*Berkshire Eagle collection*)

The worst disaster associated with the industry was the Morewood Lake Ice Co. boiler explosion in December 1910 which killed seventeen men **[B]**. Pittsfield Mayor William H. MacInnes quickly organized a relief drive and some $10,000 was raised to help the families of the dead and injured. (*Berkshire Eagle collection*)

Workers pole and push ice blocks to a conveyor to be lifted into a Sheffield storage house in 1939 **[C]**. (*James O. Saunders photo, author's collection*)

It was an icy winter in Florida in 1942 **[D]**. This chilly scene of the Baptist Church won an Associated Press contest for best picture in the small city features class for Randy Trabold (1918-80). Trabold was staff photographer for *The Transcript* in North Adams for forty-eight years. (*Berkshire Eagle collection*)

Taking pleasure in the wintry weather, skaters circle the ice at Springside Park in Pittsfield in 1942 **[E]**. (*Berkshire Eagle*)

A Sunday Afternoon on the Fields of Arrowhead

In a scene dotted with wide-skirted women seated in the grass—reminiscent of a painting by George Seurat—Allan Melville (1823-72) surveys the grounds of his Pittsfield farm Arrowhead in 1868. He chats with his brother-in-law and neighbor Col. Richard Lathers (1819-1903) of Abby Lodge. A lawyer in New York, Melville dabbled in the literary world; he acted as agent for his struggling novelist brother Herman (1819-91) in finding publishers for *The Whale* and other works. Herman Melville's short story "I and My Chimney" uses Arrowhead as a setting; the author lived and wrote there for thirteen years previous to Allan purchasing it for a summer home in 1863. Herman left to take a job at the New York customs house. After Allan Melville's death, the Holmes Road property remained in the family until 1975, when it was acquired by the Berkshire County Historical Society, which today maintains it as a house museum. (*Berkshire County Historical Society collection, thanks to Susan Eisley*)

A

B

Readers

Regional bookmobiles **[A]** have long supplied readers in city and outlying village with reading material.

Children scan books at the Morningside Branch of the Berkshire Athenaeum **[B]**. The Athenaeum incorporated in 1872 and opened its building on Park Square four years later with a collection of about 8,000 volumes. The facility was closely linked with the Berkshire Museum—for which industrialist Zenas Crane Jr. donated a new building on South Street in 1903—until they separated in 1932. The library's Tyler Street branch opened in 1942, and early visiting readers include Richard Legge, Peter Sullivan and Paul Nesbit, foreground, from St. Mary's School, and Madeline Avalle from Crane School.

During the period when Harlan Hoge Ballard (1853-1934) served as the Berkshire Athenaeum's director, the library developed its Herman Melville collection, thanks to the hard work of Ballard's assistant, Fanny G. Clark (1886-1987) **[C]**. A Pittsfield native, Clark worked at the library from 1914 to 1956, serving as assistant librarian, catalog librarian and custodian of the local history collection. She was listed in *Who's Who of American Women* in 1958. (*All Berkshire Eagle*)

C

Writers

Catharine Maria Sedgwick (1789-1867) caught the literary world by surprise with her first novel, *A New England Tale* (1822). She was the center of a literary circle which drew writers such as Ralph Waldo Emerson, Washington Irving and Nathaniel Hawthorne to Stockbridge and Lenox, earning the area the designation "American Lake District." Pictured is Sedgwick's home on Kemble Street in Lenox, now gone **[A]**. (*Lenox Historical Society, thanks to Nancy Marasco*)

Novelist Edith Newbold Jones Wharton (1862-1937) used Lenox and environs as setting in such works as *Ethan Frome*. Born to a wealthy family in New York, she summered in Newport before discovering Lenox, where she built her home The Mount—today preserved by Edith Wharton Restoration and summer home to Shakespeare & Company. A commemorative postage stamp bearing Wharton's image was issued in 1980; Lenox Postmaster Edward Barry, right, presents a large-size reproduction to Dennis Krausnick, director of Edith Wharton Restoration **[B]**. (*Photo taken and loaned by Art Marasco*)

Sinclair Lewis (1885-1951) **[C]**, the first American to win the Nobel Prize for Literature, purchased Thorvale Farm in Williamstown in 1946 and wrote *Kingsblood Royal* while living there. (*Berkshire Eagle collection, courtesy Samuel E. Allen*).

Edna St. Vincent Millay (1892-1950) **[D]** made her summer home at Steepletop in Austerlitz, N.Y. She was the first woman poet to win the Pulitzer Prize, for *The Harp-Weaver and Other Poems* in 1923. (*Berkshire Eagle collection, courtesy Morgan Bulkeley by permission of Norma Millay*)

Gerard Chapman **[E]** worked as a chemical engineer before taking over his father William's Chicago-based fiction story syndicate in 1945. Now a Lee resident, Chapman became keenly interested in local history, writing "Our Berkshires" columns for *The Berkshire Eagle* for two decades beginning in 1977. (*Berkshire Eagle collection, Marie Tassone photo*)

Media

Newsrooms are seldom this quiet **[A]**. *The Berkshire Eagle's* sports editor, Joseph Adrian Pfeiffer (1886-1919), and city editor, Clarence A. "Doc" Crandall (1879-1960), ready stories for the Sept. 10, 1916, issue. Pfeiffer was on the *Eagle* staff for thirteen years. Crandall, a Hancock native, joined the newspaper in 1898 and remained for forty-eight years. Covering the city beat, he had a broad knowledge of topics ranging from ornithology and horticulture to religion, jurisprudence, meteorology and filinophilia (fear of cats). He was also adept at shorthand. His last big story was the 1944 John F. Noxon murder trial. (*Matt Powell/Berkshire Eagle*)

WBEC radio announcer Dana Jones **[B]** holds newscast copy in his teeth while he adjusts the volume on his morning program and cues a recording. The station's original disc jockey when it went on air in 1947, Jones later became program director. (*William Mahan/Berkshire Eagle, 1957*)

Engineer Oscar G. Brandt **[C]** adjusts a television receiver to pick up the first broadcast image in the Berkshires in September 1944 at Bascom Lodge atop Mount Greylock. Six people witnessed on the circular screen a crisp image of the surrender of the Germans in Paris. (*Arthur Palme/Berkshire Eagle*)

Communications

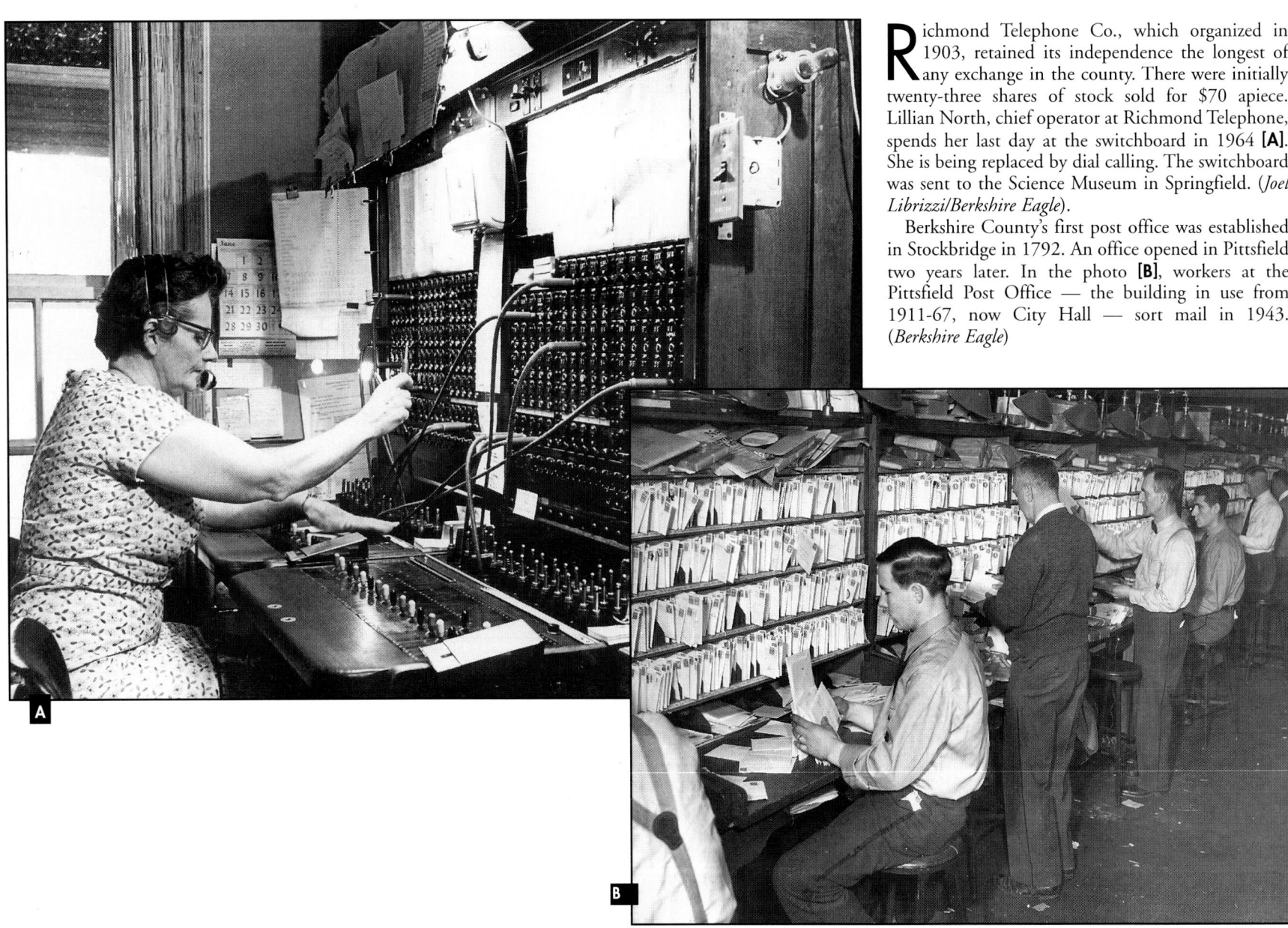

Richmond Telephone Co., which organized in 1903, retained its independence the longest of any exchange in the county. There were initially twenty-three shares of stock sold for $70 apiece. Lillian North, chief operator at Richmond Telephone, spends her last day at the switchboard in 1964 **[A]**. She is being replaced by dial calling. The switchboard was sent to the Science Museum in Springfield. (*Joel Librizzi/Berkshire Eagle*).

Berkshire County's first post office was established in Stockbridge in 1792. An office opened in Pittsfield two years later. In the photo **[B]**, workers at the Pittsfield Post Office — the building in use from 1911-67, now City Hall — sort mail in 1943. (*Berkshire Eagle*)

Artists

Daniel Chester French (1850-1931) **[A]** and daughter Margaret French Cresson (1889-1957) are in front of his studio in the Glendale section of Stockbridge in the late 1920s. French, whose sculptures include the Minute Man in Concord and the seated Abraham Lincoln at the Memorial in Washington, D.C, summered at Chesterwood, a property which today is maintained as a museum by the National Trust for Historic Preservation. Cresson was herself a prize-winning sculptor, among her subjects the explorer Admiral Richard Byrd. (*Berkshire Eagle collection, C.S. Hayward*)

Sheffield graphic artist Seymour "Rob" Robins **[B]** has designed dozens of paper sculptures including a functional armillary sphere which was commissioned by the Smithsonian Institution in 1970. The Ontario native said his works are included in the permanent collection of the Cooper-Hewitt National Design Museum in New York City. (*Bernard Drew photo*)

Painter and sculptor Alexander Stirling Calder (1898-1976) **[C]** summered in Richmond, where his father, sculptor Alexander Milne Calder (1846-1923), owned a home on Swamp Road from 1926-40. The elder Calder's commissions included the statue of William Penn for Philadelphia City Hall. The younger Calder created wire sculptures and innovative mobiles, early examples of which are among holdings of the Berkshire Museum in Pittsfield. (*Berkshire Eagle collection*)

Michael McCurdy **[D]**, working at his press in this self-portrait, has won awards for his wood engravings and scratchboards. The Great Barrington artist's drawings have accompanied the works of authors ranging from Louisa May Alcott and L. Frank Baum to Donald Hall and David Mamet. (*Courtesy Michael McCurdy*)

An artistic tradition, albeit amateur, is Halloween window painting in Great Barrington **[E]**. This trio completes an ephemeral masterpiece in October 1951. (*Great Barrington Historical Society, Marie Tassone collection*)

Stage

Actress Katherine De Mille makes her Berkshire Playhouse debut in Stockbridge in 1936 in "Topaze" [A]. The adopted daughter of director Cecil B. De Mille, she strived for success without relying on the family name. She later appeared in a number of films and married (and divorced) actor Anthony Quinn.

Crackerbox humorist and Lanesboro native Josh Billings, a.k.a. Henry Wheeler Shaw (1818-85), is one of the characters depicted in a tableau staged by the Pomona Grange in Lanesboro in 1938 [B]. John Cornhill plays Josh, Mrs. Nelson Hinman is Lady Lanesborough and Milton J. Miller plays Jonathan Smith, the plain farmer.

Rowena Humphrey of Worthington won the title when she walked onto the stage in the 1978 Miss Massachusetts competition and performed a self-choreographed ballet to the theme from *Love Story*. She is at the time a sophomore at Berkshire Community College and living with her brother in Dalton [C]. (*All Berkshire Eagle collection*)

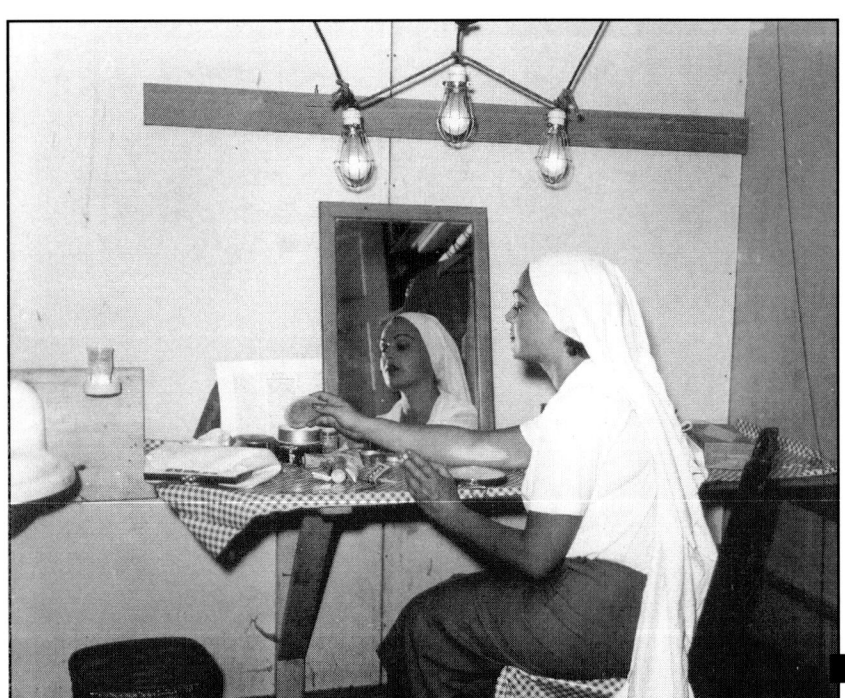

Mrs. Will Toennies is on the left, Margery Whiting is on the right, and the woman in the center is unidentified [D]. They are playing roles in a Boltwood-Liddle operetta. Librettist Edward Boltwood (1880-1934) and composer Fred J. Liddle (1858-1914) authored four musical shows which were staged locally from 1904-12. The first, "A Happy Day," was performed both at Pittsfield's Colonial Theater (now an art supply store which a group of citizens hopes to restore for performances) and at Great Barrington's Mahaiwe Theater (which still shows motion pictures) in 1904. (*Berkshire Eagle collection, courtesy Anne Whiting*)

Lenox Town Hall hosts a charity performance by the social group which called itself Kermis in September 1906 [E]. (*Berkshire Eagle collection*)

The Social Eight minstrel performers from perhaps the early 1900s [F] consist of W.P. Cushman, Henry Brace, Martin Mallory, Frank Kearney, M.J. Kelleher, P.H. O'Donnell and (not shown) W. Kelleher and W. Harvey. (*Berkshire Eagle collection, courtesy Mrs. Robert Hickey*)

Out of Context

That face looks familiar; but is he a farmer? Does he usually play the piano? Does she always do garden work? The girls seen way out of context are Bette and Barbara Davis **[A]**, students at a private school in the Berkshire section of Lanesboro in 1919-20. Bette (1908-89) went on to become a Hollywood actress. On a swing through the area in 1934 she paid a return visit to see Marjorie Whiting (1886-1943), headmaster of Crestalban School for Girls from 1917-43, and her brother Henry Whiting and his wife Evelyn, who ran Crestalban Farm and Camp. (*Berkshire Eagle, courtesy Anne Whiting*)

Aaron Copland (1900-90) **[B]**, composer of *Appalachian Spring*, steers a tractor around his Richmond summer place in about 1960. "There was something about the sound of music that fascinated me...," Copland said in a 1980 interview. "When I told my father I wanted to be a composer of concert music, he said, 'Where did you get such an idea?' He was concerned whether I could make a living at it." Copland taught at the Berkshire Music Center in Lenox some twenty-five years. (*Berkshire Eagle collection, H.R. Birt photo*)

Playwright William Gibson **[C]** takes a turn at the ivories. The Stockbridge resident's credits include *Two for the Seesaw* (1956) and *The Miracle Worker* (1960), which were staged in New York City and made into motion pictures. Before these successes, during his struggling early years of writing, he supplemented his income by teaching piano. (*Berkshire Eagle, 1968*)

George Herman "Babe" Ruth (1895-1948) trades bat for shotgun when he visits Russell Whitbeck's deer camp in Mount Washington, circa 1940 **[D]**. "The Sultan of Swat," one of the all-time best known baseball players, hit a record-shattering sixty home runs during the 1927 season. Whitbeck (1891-1964) was superintendent of Mount Everett Reservation for thirty-four years, retiring in 1961. (*Berkshire Eagle collection*)

Actress Julie Harris (b. 1925) and her then-husband, theatrical producer Manning Gurion, tend the grounds of their Williamsville home **[E]**. The Tony and Emmy award winner established herself as a stage actress in 1950, appearing in *The Member of the Wedding* on Broadway and repeating the role in the movie version. (*Great Barrington Historical Society, Marie Tassone collection*)

The Berkshire Street Railway's 1903 luxury "Berkshire Hills" parlor car, built by Wason Manufacturing of Springfield, carried passengers from Great Barrington to Bennington, Vt. After it was decommissioned in the 1920s, it became a diner in West Pittsfield **[F]**, and eventually was incorporated into the Coach Lite restaurant. Heavily damaged by fire in 1994, it is now at the Seashore Trolley Museum in Maine. (*Berkshire Eagle collection, C.S. Hayward photo*)

Music

Conductor Serge Koussevitzky (1874-1951) with guest Eleanor Roosevelt (1884-1962) and the Boston Symphony Orchestra rehearse for a performance of *Peter and the Wolf* at Tanglewood in Stockbridge in 1950 **[A]**. The first Berkshire Symphonic Festival featured a program by the New York Philharmonic and was held at the Dan Hanna Farm (now DeSisto School) in Interlaken. The summer series moved to its permanent home at the former Tappan estate in 1937. (*Berkshire Eagle*)

Gertrude Robinson Smith (1881-1963) **[B]** was founder of the Berkshire Symphonic Festival in 1934 and its president until it dissolved in 1955. She sparked a fund drive to construct the Music Shed at Tanglewood. During World War I, Smith was chairwoman of the flotilla committee of the Vacation War Relief in New York. She raised more than $100,000 to provide ice-making machines at the front, helping save the lives of numerous wounded soldiers. The French Republic elected her to the French Legion of Honor as a chevalier and later as an officer. Her father held the same standing, and they were the only father-daughter combination in this country. (*Berkshire Eagle*)

Arlo Guthrie, a resident of the town of Washington, early in his folk music career performed for a Channel 2 benefit in Pittsfield, backed up by a house band consisting of Albert P. Nolli Sr. (1921-84), Albert P. Nolli Jr. and Stanley "Stash" Duzlak (1919-88), in September 1972 **[C]**. Do you suppose they gave the "You can get anything you want at Alice's Restaurant" chorus a polka beat? Both Nolli Sr., who worked for the Pittsfield Sanitation Department for thirty years, and Duzlak, who worked for GE's Power Transformer Department for thirty-nine years, had their own bands, the Al Nolli Trio and the Stash Duzlak Band, respectively. (*Glenn Boyd photo, courtesy Donna Drew*)

The K.O. Davis Piano Shop [D] operated from 1944-58 on Elm Street in Pittsfield. Kenneth O. Davis (1907-1989), a science professor at North Adams State College, also repaired and tuned pianos. A one-time member of the Berkshire Symphony, Davis "had absolute pitch," his wife Marie Davis said. "He could strike any article and he knew right off what key it was in." Mrs. Davis ran the business, which she said started as a piano store but ended up selling all kinds of instruments. (*Courtesy Marie Davis*)

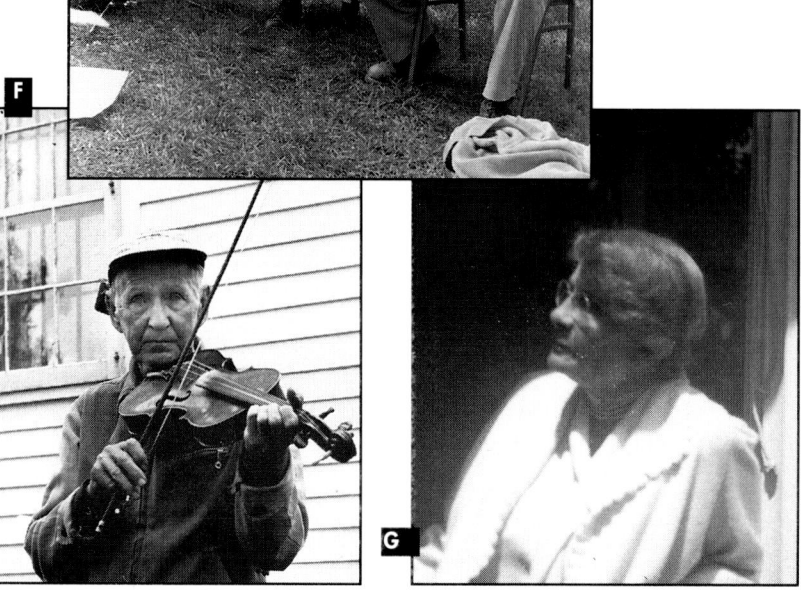

The Big Waaagh Scratch Band [E] performs, as one writer described it, "hot gonzo world music" or possibly "acoustic traditional boogie." Members Adam Rothberg on strings, Morgan Rael on steel drum, Anita "Nattie" Carroll on accordion and Thomas "Tom Jawbone" Weldon on vocals and limberjack perform at the Berkshire Botanical Garden. Established as the Berkshire Garden Center in Stockbridge in 1934 by Irene Botsford Hoffman (1877-1960), who served as its president until 1941, the facility hosts a harvest festival each autumn featuring crafts, activities and music. (*Bernard Drew photo, 1993*)

George R. "Pop" Sweet (1884-1965) [F], born in Peru and in later years a resident of Becket, was the self-named "King of Country Fiddlers." He called his first square dance when he was fourteen and living in Lee. With his band, the Huckleberry Pickers, he performed far and wide. Sweet sometimes played his fiddle the hard way—behind his neck, or under his leg—and once scratched out a tune on a section of stove pipe. (*Berkshire Eagle, 1961*)

Elizabeth Sprague Coolidge (1864-1953) [G], "the fairy godmother of chamber music," for four decades devoted her energies to promoting the sounds she loved. The daughter of the president of a wholesale grocery corporation, she came to Pittsfield in 1904 with her husband Dr. Frederick S. Coolidge, an orthopedic surgeon who had been forced to retire prematurely because of ill health. In 1915, Mrs. Coolidge formed the Berkshire Quartet, among whose members was Willem Willeke (1880-1950), noted cellist who later served as director of the South Mountain Temple of Chamber Music which Mrs. Coolidge built in 1917-18. (*Berkshire Eagle, 1938*)

Henry Doll (1868-1916) formed a ten-member marching band [H] in Adams in 1892 which evolved into the Germania Band, the first musical group to give a performance atop Mount Greylock, July 17, 1904. They played morning and afternoon concerts featuring Sousa's march "Hail to the Spirit of Liberty," Offenbach's overture from "Orpheus" and other selections. (*Adams Historical Society collection, thanks to Eugene F. Michalenko*)

125

Dancers

World-famous dancer Ted Shawn (1891-1972), founder-director of Jacob's Pillow Dance Festival, met his future partner and wife Ruth St. Denis in 1914. They started a school in New York and licensed Denishawn schools all over the country. The couple separated in 1931, but remained married. Shawn the next year purchased the Arthur E. Morgan farm in Becket and it became home to his famed company of men dancers [A], shown here in the final pose from "Polonaise" in 1936. (*Jacob's Pillow collection, Richard Merrill photo, thanks to Norton Owen*)

Shawn's Men's Group disbanded in 1940 and the next year the dancer established the festival at Jacob's Pillow. He engaged engineer Joseph Franz (1882-1959) of Stockbridge to design a theater; they inspect the construction in progress in this photo from 1942 [B]. (*Jacob's Pillow collection, thanks to Norton Owen*)

St. Denis (1878?-1968) [C] began her career as a dancer in New York in 1894, doing eleven shows a day at Worth's Museum on 30th Street for $20 a week. At the height of her career, during the late 1920s, she and Shawn commanded upwards of $3,500 a week. (*Berkshire Eagle collection, White Studio*)

The Oasis YMCA nightclub in Pittsfield [D] attracts more than 1,000 people one Saturday night in January, 1944. Napoleon Reid (1926-87), in the foreground, a freshman at Pittsfield High School and a football player, was later a member of the Pittsfield Redevelopment Authority and a vigorous proponent of low-income housing. (*Berkshire Eagle*)

Photographers

This book wouldn't have been possible without the efforts of dozens of photographers, professional and amateur. Anson Clark of West Stockbridge (1783-1847) was Berkshire's first camera man, opening a Daguerreotype shop in West Stockbridge in 1841. This advertisement for Clark's studio **[A]** ran in *The Berkshire Courier* in May that year. Perhaps the single most historic photo taken by Clark was of Agrippa Hull (1759-1848), an African-American who was six years in service during the Revolutionary War as body servant to Gen. Thaddeus Kosciusko. The 1844 Daguerreotype image has faded and is unprintable today; it did provide the basis for an oil painting of Hull, however, which is in the collection of the Stockbridge Local History Room.

O.B. and E.W. Buell had photography studios in Pittsfield and Great Barrington and were adept at portraits and landscapes, the latter often sold as stereo slides. The Buell portable darkroom is seen on Main Street, Great Barrington, in the 1870s. **[B]** (*Mason Library collection, thanks to Marlene L. Drew*)

Pittsfield resident Edwin Hale Lincoln (1848-1938), a Civil War veteran and photographer of Berkshire flora and of Berkshire estates, works in his darkroom in 1936 **[C]**. (*Berkshire Eagle collection*)

Pioneer photojournalist Stefan Lorant (1901-97) **[D]** of Lenox was a foremost Abraham Lincoln historian. Born in Budapest, Hungary, he was editor of the magazine *Munich Illustrated* when jailed by Adolf Hitler in the 1930s. Lorant came to America in 1940. Among his books was *Pittsburgh: The Story of an American City*. Art Marasco, who took this picture, was Pentagon photographer from 1950-52 (his subjects included Dwight D. Eisenhower, Queen Elizabeth and Winston Churchill) and later established a studio in Lenox. (*Courtesy Art Marasco*)

Will Plouffe, Photographer

Pittsfield's Will Plouffe bears strong resemblance, in the self-portrait [A], to Casey the Crime Photographer. Plouffe took up photography as a Boy Scout and hasn't put down his camera in the seventy or so years since. A Pittsfield native, Plouffe sold his first photo to *The Berkshire Eagle* in 1933, earning $2. It was of the Memorial Day parade. While a high school student, he developed rolls of film and made prints for neighbors and friends. Photo finishing for drugstores, he earned enough in nine months to buy his first German Zeiss camera.

Plouffe was a staff photographer for General Electric for four years before opening his own studio on Fenn Street in 1946—the first electronic flash studio in the city. He was often in the darkroom making prints late into the night, Plouffe explained, and he was called on to take pictures for the local police and fire departments. He became night photographer for *The Eagle*. He garnered a National Press Photographers Association award for his photo of a fire at Berkshire Woolen Mill on Pecks Road in 1953 [B].

His studio's busiest years, Plouffe said, were immediately after World War II, when returning soldiers were eager to marry. Plouffe and one other photographer in Pittsfield did about 125 weddings each a year. Plouffe said he wore out the shutters on two Speed Graphics the two seasons he was official Tanglewood photographer. With the growing popularity of the 35mm camera, however, the photographer found his studio business diminishing and he closed it. He became staff photographer for E.D. Jones before retiring. That's his wife Irma in the scene from Monument Mountain in Great Barrington [C]. (*All courtesy Will Plouffe*)